PRAISE
HAB

D0020819

"This autobiography by a millennial Helen Keller teems with grace and grit."

—*O, The Oprah Magazine*

"HABEN is…a profoundly important memoir. Engaging and amusing, Girma…is a talented narrator who captures defining moments in her life in a series of lyrical cameos. She writes with remarkable assurance and yet with a lightness of touch when tackling difficult issues. Her book is primarily an essay on disability and on the determination needed to conquer discrimination and exclusion. In a characteristically challenging passage, Girma observes that 'Someday the world will learn that people with disabilities are talented, too.' With the publication of her autobiography, no reader could sensibly doubt that day has come."

—*The Times*

"A stirring memoir of love and resilience. Haben proves there are no limits for living joyously in the world. A fierce, glorious advocate for equal opportunity, she demonstrates that accessibility for all benefits all. Her memoir is a soul-inspiring gift."

—Jewell Parker Rhodes, *New York Times* bestselling author of *Ghost Boys*

"Riveting…[an] often hilarious and utterly inspiring memoir."

—*BookPage* (starred review)

"Reading Haben's story moved me in a way I didn't think was possible. She's a gifted writer, and her story will teach you about strength, perseverance, and determination. This is a strong reminder to embrace the unknown, to stand up for yourself, and to never give up."

—Mashal Waqar, co-founder and COO, The Tempest

"Extraordinary...Haben's is a story of inspiration—and new American patriotism. She gives all of us fresh strength and hope."

—Lorene Cary, author of *Black Ice* and founder of Art Sanctuary

"What makes Haben's prodigious story even more remarkable is that she's not satisfied with being inspiring. Because she knows that achievement only happens when there is more than the support of individual extraordinary people, she pushes institutions and leaders in the academy, the government, and in big tech to widen the corridors of power and opportunity. Her intersectional approach to her work as an advocate for the disabled and as a Deafblind daughter of refugees refuses tokenization and demands true inclusion."

—dream hampton, award-winning filmmaker, writer, and organizer

"With wit and passion, Haben...takes readers through her often unaccommodating world. This is a heartwarming memoir of a woman who champions access and dignity for all."

—*Publishers Weekly* (starred review)

Haben

The Deafblind Woman
Who Conquered Harvard Law

Haben Girma

TWELVE

New York Boston

Twelve
Hachette Book Group
1290 Avenue of the Americas, New York, NY 10104
twelvebooks.com
twitter.com/twelvebooks

Originally published in hardcover and ebook by Twelve in August 2019.

First Trade Edition: August 2020

Twelve is an imprint of Grand Central Publishing. The Twelve name and logo are trademarks of Hachette Book Group, Inc.

The publisher is not responsible for websites (or their content) that are not owned by the publisher.

The Hachette Speakers Bureau provides a wide range of authors for speaking events. To find out more, go to www.hachettespeakersbureau.com or call (866) 376-6591.

Library of Congress Cataloging-in-Publication Data
Names: Girma, Haben, 1988-, author.
Title: Haben: The Deafblind Woman Who Conquered Harvard Law / By Haben Girma.
Description: New York: Twelve, 2019.
Identifiers: LCCN 2018050294| ISBN 9781538728727 (hardcover) | ISBN 9781478992813 (audio download) | ISBN 9781538728710 (ebook)
Subjects: LCSH: Girma, Haben, 1988- | Lawyers with disabilities—United States—Biography. | Women lawyers—United States—Biography.
Classification: LCC KF373.G567 A3 2019 | DDC 340.092 [B]—dc23
LC record available at https://lccn.loc.gov/2018050294

ISBNs: 978-1-5387-2873-4 (trade pbk.), 978-1-5387-2871-0 (ebook)

Printed in the United States of America

LSC-C

10 9 8 7 6 5 4 3 2 1

Contents

Contents

*"The best and most beautiful
things in the world cannot be
seen or even touched. They must
be felt with the heart."*
—*Helen Keller*

Introduction

I'm Deafblind. Because I can't see faces or recognize voices, every conversation needs to start with a name. My friends begin conversations like this: "It's Cam," "It's Gordon," or if someone is drinking, "It's me."

My name is Haben. "Ha" like ha-ha, and "ben" like benevolent.

Deafblindness encompasses a spectrum of vision and hearing loss, from the guy squinting at conversations signed three feet in front of his face, to the woman pounding the pavement with her white cane while analyzing traffic sounds through her hearing aids. I was born Deafblind. At age twelve I could walk into a room and see the indistinct outline of a person sitting on top of the long, blurred shape of a couch. That image fades more and more every year. Now, walking into a room is like stepping into an abstract painting of fuzzy formations and colorful splashes.

My hearing follows a similar path. I was born with poor low frequency hearing and good high frequency hearing. Speech intelligence relies on high frequency consonants, so I intuitively learned to speak at a high vocal register. At age twelve I could hear my parents if they sat next to me and spoke slowly and clearly. Now, we communicate with the assistance of technology, such as a keyboard paired with a braille computer.

Communities designed with just one kind of person in mind isolate those of us defying their narrow definition of personhood. This book takes readers on a quest for connection across the world, including building a school under the scorching Malian sun, climbing icebergs in Alaska, training with a guide dog in New Jersey, studying law at Harvard, and sharing a magical moment with President Obama at the White House. Unlike most memoirs, the stories here unfold in present tense. Hindsight may be 20/20, but 20/20 is not how I experience this ever-surprising world.

Chapter One

When They Took My Father

Addis Ababa, Ethiopia. Summer 1995.

Two men in uniforms stand in the aisle of the plane, towering over Daddy. I watch from the seat next to him, straining to see the shadowy figures. Their curt tones trigger the sensation of mosquitos stabbing my skin.

Daddy unbuckles his seatbelt. "I have to go," he tells me.

The two men escort him off the plane. For the first time in my seven-year-old life, I'm alone.

I stare down the aisle. My field of vision ends at around five feet. A person walks by wheeling a bag. Two kids go by with backpacks.

I sink into my seat and close my eyes. This plane is supposed to take us to London, then another plane will get us back to America. I was born and raised in Oakland, California. Daddy grew up in Ethiopia, so we came here for the summer. My mom and sister plan to enjoy two more weeks of vacation before returning to the United States.

Memories from the summer play through my mind: dancing on the dusty streets with my sister and the neighborhood kids, baking raisin bread with Mommy, swimming in the Red Sea with Daddy...

My eyes open. I stare down the aisle again. No one walks by. Everyone has boarded.

It's been an hour. Why isn't he back?

An invisible chain of tension squeezes my throat. The pain climbs up my neck to my head. I take deep breaths, struggling to hold on to hope.

An announcement blasts through the PA system. The sound washes over me in incoherent murmurs, accelerating my pulse to a dizzying clip.

All my life I've heard stories of Ethiopian soldiers tearing families apart. Soldiers threw Mommy in jail just for refusing to sing a song. Ethiopia claimed the neighboring country Eritrea, and for thirty years Eritreans fought for independence. Daddy was born and raised in Ethiopia, but his father, Grandpa Kidane, is Eritrean. During the war, Eritreans living in Ethiopia became targets. The war ended in 1991, though. It's supposed to be safe for Eritreans visiting Ethiopia. Why did they take Daddy?

The thought demolishes me like a kick to the stomach. I gasp for air as the pain spreads through my body.

Why didn't our American citizenship stop them from separating us?

My eyes study his empty seat. He's gone. I touch the seat, even though I already know. He's gone. My hand feels a seatbelt. His seatbelt. The long smooth strap contrasts with

4

the sharp metal buckle, the buckle that failed to keep him safe.

Strong vibrations shake the jet. The engines rattle every nerve from the soles of my feet to the back of my neck.

Burning pain tightens around my chest, climbing all the way up to my cheekbones. Breathing hurts. My nose labors for air as I fight against the suffocating fear.

I need Daddy. Who will help me navigate the world? I don't know how to find my next flight when we land in London. I don't even know the international number to reach Mommy.

A flight attendant looms over my seat. Mumble, mumble, mumble. She drops to my level. Mumble, mumble, mumble.

Terror clamps my mouth shut. Pain immobilizes every muscle. The only movement comes from my tears.

The flight attendant speaks again. Mumble, mumble, mumble.

I stare at her, begging her to hear my thoughts. Bring back Daddy.

She rises to her full height, turns, and disappears.

Another flight attendant stands at the head of the aisle. From her gestures I know she's going over the safety procedures. Too late. My life has already crashed.

My hands squeeze the seatbelt Daddy used. That's when I discover moisture on the metal buckle.

A person rushes up the aisle, lunging into the seat next to mine. He's back!

I take a small breath, and pain shoots through my jaw as my body struggles to relax.

Nothing can truly shield me from the violence of the world.

Not my family, not American citizenship, not even self-defense classes for blind kids. At any moment, the forces of the world could take the lives of the people I love. They could even snatch mine.

When we arrive in London, Daddy leads the way to our next gate. We settle into our seats, waiting for our flight to America. I gather the courage to finally ask, "Why did they take you off the plane?"

"I don't know. It's okay now, though."

I shake my head. "Tell me. I can handle it."

He picks up a magazine from the seat next to him and flips through the pages. "I don't know. I honestly don't understand it."

"That's okay...Then what happened?"

He sighs. "They asked me if I was the son of Kidane. I told them yes. Then they asked me to fill out some paperwork. The plane was about to leave, so when the guy wasn't looking I just ran for it."

My eyes water. "I'm glad you made it back."

He wraps his arm around my shoulders. "Me, too, Habeniye."

Chapter Two

The Expeditions Begin

Oakland, California. Fall 2000.

"I hate to say this, kiddo, but you're failing the class."

My Deaf ears doubt what they hear. I look up at Ms. Scott, a teacher I trust and admire. We're in the resource room for blind students at Bret Harte Middle School. The classroom offers the school's blind students—all seven of us—braille books, braille typewriters, a braille embosser, computers with assistive software, magnifiers, even braille versions of Monopoly and UNO. We take turns working in the resource room for one period each day. The rest of the time we attend regular, mainstream classes with our nondisabled classmates.

Ms. Scott and her assistants help mainstream teachers with accessibility, converting reading assignments to braille, audio, or large print, depending on the needs of the student. They also provide blindness training: identifying coins by touch, folding cash bills to tell them apart, and using the internet with magnification or text-to-speech software.

Ms. Scott sits down next to me and tries again. "Mr. Smith asked me to braille your marking period report. I'm going to braille it for you, but I figured we'd talk about it now. It says you haven't completed many of your homework assignments."

"But I did all the assignments, all the homework." My stomach twists with indignation.

"I'm just telling you what it says on the paper."

"I always do my homework. I've never missed an assignment. Maybe this is someone else's report?"

"I'm sorry, Haben, but it has your name on it."

Kicking the ground, I sit up straighter in my chair. "Then I don't know. This doesn't make any sense. I did all the work."

"It's okay, kiddo. I'm on your team. I know you work hard. Let's just talk this through. Do you remember not doing at least one assignment?"

"No. I wouldn't do that."

"I don't think you would, either. Why don't we ask Mr. Smith about this?"

I nod, too anxious to speak. My subconscious buzzes with a warning. Something about Mr. Smith's class puts me on edge.

"I'll call and see if he's in now." Ms. Scott walks over to her desk. Her voice sounds muffled now as she speaks outside of my hearing range.

My hands drop to the braille book in front of me. Nancy Drew, a brilliant woman with the courage to stride into terrifying situations, is one of my heroes. My fingers glide across the dots, following her on one of her adventures. The story distracts me from the fear clawing at my spine.

Ms. Scott returns to the table. "He's free now. Shall we head over?"

My jaw clamps shut again. Standing on hesitant legs, I follow her out the door.

She turns left, moving down a hallway with a musty old-building smell. My heart thuds against my ribs as I trudge behind her. We soon cross a courtyard where the breeze carries a whiff of eucalyptus, and the scent reminds me of the decongestant my family uses on miserable, stuffy nose days.

She slows to walk beside me. "How are the cartwheels?"

A small smile flickers on my face. When I told her my dream of finally mastering the cartwheel, she volunteered to help. We spent a whole period at the school gym practicing. Haben, kick your legs higher! Keep your legs straight! Keep trying!

"I can't quite get my legs straight over my head."

"You were getting close the other day. Keep practicing. I know you can do it."

I blush, embarrassed. Another blind student has been cartwheeling since fourth grade. Ms. Scott has known how to cartwheel for more than twenty years. Then there's me, twelve years old and cartwheel-challenged. "I'll practice," I mumble.

Ms. Scott really is a phenomenal teacher, peppering our lessons with all kinds of surprises. Last year she introduced me to hot cider, which tastes divine, and eggnog, which tastes vile. She helped me register with the National Braille and Talking Book Library, and taught me how to order *Harry Potter*. The middle school has a tiny braille library, so I need access to the national library.

She breezes through Mr. Smith's open door and stops by his desk. I stop beside her.

Mr. Smith talks as he approaches. His words blur together into an inaudible rumble.

"Are you serious?" Ms. Scott asks.

Mumble, mumble. His response sounds like German. Some of his speech sounds come through, enough to know that he's speaking. But not enough to identify the words.

"No way!" She bursts into laughter.

My knees tremble. Are they laughing at me? I look from one to the other, straining to hear.

Mr. Smith clears his throat. "So how can I help you?"

"Haben has a question for you," Ms. Scott tells him.

"Yes?" The tall silhouette stands before me, waiting.

I swallow. "The report says I'm missing assignments, but I did turn in all the assignments."

"Can I see that?" He takes the paper from Ms. Scott. "There are about ten missing. Did you read and respond to the questions for chapter four?"

"I…I thought you skipped chapter four."

He gives an inaudible response.

"I'm wondering," Ms. Scott jumps in. "How do you assign homework?"

"I usually write it on the board, but I read it out loud, too."

"Okay." She thinks for a bit. "Are you standing in the front of the room when you read it out loud?"

"It depends on where I am at the time. Sometimes I call out the assignment from my desk."

"Haben, can you hear him from his desk?"

I shake my head. My seat is at the front of the class facing the board. Mr. Smith usually stands or sits in the front of the class. His desk is all the way in the back of the room near the door.

"So that's what's going on. She didn't know about those assignments because she didn't hear them." Ms. Scott's voice sounds calm, nonjudgmental. "Haben, what are some things you can do to make sure you get the assignment?"

"Umm...I could ask one of the students at the end of class...I could ask Mr. Smith..."

She turns the question to him. "Do you think that could work?"

"Sure. You can come ask me if you have any questions. I do have a question for you, though. Why don't you use hearing aids?"

"They don't work for my type of hearing loss. I've tried them." My throat tightens in dread. My audiologist explained that because my hearing loss is the opposite of the typical type of hearing loss, the hearing aids on the market aren't designed to help me. People believe her, but when they hear it from me they wonder if I'm just being a stubborn preteen.

"Gotcha," he says.

Silence.

"Haben," Ms. Scott says, "did you want to ask about making up those assignments you missed?"

"Is that possible?" My voice rises with hope. "Can I turn them in late and still get credit?"

"Sure. If you finish them by next Friday you can get credit for them."

"I'll do it. Thanks."

Back in the resource room, Ms. Scott takes charge. "All right, kiddo. I'm going to braille this list for you—have a seat." She walks over to the computer next to the braille embosser. The computer has software that converts print to braille, and then sends that information to an embosser. The embosser punches dots into thick paper, producing braille.

I slip into a chair, fold my arms on the table, and rest my head. The visit with Mr. Smith wiped me out. Apparently, assuming teachers will always give me the information I need leads to failure. If I want to succeed, I'll have to work to gain access to every visual detail and every spoken word. Every single time.

Three hours later I'm back in Mr. Smith's history class. Sitting at my desk, my fingers fly across the braille book in front of me. Every line, every word, every letter touches my fingertips and instantly enters my mind. No strain. No pain. The physicality makes reading a whole-body experience.

Part of me knows I'm missing a student reading, and the sound of thirty kids fidgeting in their seats. Thirty faces peering into identical books. Perhaps a few even sneak glances at one another. I know millions of sights and sounds are playing out on the streets of Oakland at this very moment. The sensory-scape continues around the world—the reddish brown of Redwood bark. The radiant glow of Big Ben at night. The majestic roar of Victoria Falls. The swell of voices in Singapore's streets. Tastes and smells and textures, too. The world's a steaming sensory stew.

I like my Deafblind world. It's comfortable, familiar. It doesn't feel small or limited. It's all I've known; it's my normal.

Ring! The school bells mark the end of the class. The room bursts into a cacophony of kids scraping chairs, shoving papers into bags, and shouting plans across the room.

Putting my book in my backpack, I get ready to leave. Wait, is there homework? I didn't hear any homework, so there's no homework tonight, right? If I didn't hear it, then it didn't happen. If I didn't see it, then it didn't matter. Right?

My back tenses. When I told Ms. Scott I would ask another student for the homework, I failed to consider how that feels. I don't have friends here. I don't feel wanted; I just feel tolerated. Asking someone to tell me the homework will just confirm their low expectations.

Pushing past my dread, I plan to do it anyway. A student sits right behind me, so I turn around in my seat. She's standing up and preparing to leave. The noise makes it impossible for me to hear her, so I keep it short. "Bye."

The students leave. The room quiets. I slide out of my seat. Part of me knows I should walk over to the teacher and ask if he assigned any homework. Another part of me wants to escape before he assigns me homework. I don't want homework, but I don't want to fall further behind on assignments.

As I approach his desk, I scan the room for a tall figure. Nothing. I stop by his desk. Nothing. Every cell in my body tells me to run. I force myself to use my voice, "Hello?" Nothing.

My knees feel weak. I consider putting my backpack down since I don't know how long I'll have to wait. When I told Ms. Scott I would ask for the homework, I failed to consider the emotional drain of trying to find someone when you can't see or hear them.

A tall figure strides over from the other side of the room. "Are you here for the homework?"

"Yes. Is there an assignment today?"

"Read chapter eighteen and answer questions one through four."

"Okay. Thanks." I exit with my shoulders slumped, weighed down by my heavy backpack.

It's a sighted, hearing classroom, in a sighted, hearing school, in a sighted, hearing society. They designed this environment for people who can see and hear. In this environment, I'm disabled. They place the burden on me to step out of my world and reach into theirs.

Chapter Three

War

Asmara, Eritrea. Summer 2001.

The smell of home-brewed coffee fills the living room of my grandmother's house in Asmara, Eritrea. The smoke of the roasting coffee beans swirls through the living room and slips out the open windows. After roasting the beans in a pan, Grandma Awiye boils the brew in a *jebena*, a traditional Eritrean coffeepot. The ceramic vessel has a spherical base, long neck, and a short handle to grasp while pouring the potent liquid.

The room buzzes with the happy chatter of coffee time. I'm twelve years old, sitting on the sofa with my parents. My father's name is Girma. It's also my surname. Eritreans and Ethiopians traditionally use the father's first name for the child's last name. *Girma* means "charisma" and is pronounced *Ghir-mī* ("my") in Tigrinya, the language of Eritrea, and *Ghir-ma* in Amharic, the language of Ethiopia. We pronounce it both ways. My mother's name is Saba. She's named after the queen of Sheba, the revered ruler who journeyed to ancient Jerusalem on a quest for knowledge. Legend has it that all Eritreans and Ethiopians descend from King Solomon and the queen of Sheba. People tell me Saba looks like a queen.

The room bursts into uproarious laughter. The sofa cushions shake from my parents' amusement. The conversation continues, animated voices bouncing from person to person around me.

Seven other family members sit around the room. TT, my nine-year-old sister, assists Grandma Awiye with the coffee. My aunts Roma, Selam, Senait, Hiwet, and Elsa keep the conversations going. Grandma Awiye, Aunt Hiwet, and Uncle Teme live in this house year-round. Elsa now lives in the Netherlands, and the rest of us live in the United States. We try to have family reunions in Asmara every three years.

An aunt laughs, the sound rising and falling like a bird song. It piques my curiosity, leaving me longing to join the conversation. I can't identify the words in the babble of noise. The speech sounds tangle together like hair strands caught in gum. Try to pull a strand free and another strand gets caught. The mix of languages compounds the problem. Seventy percent is Tigrinya, fifteen percent is Amharic, and the rest is English.

I feel bored. A confusing, I'm-lonely-even-though-I'm-surrounded-by-people bored. I tug on Saba's arm. "Can I go?"

"No, I want you to stay with me. Why don't you talk with us?"

"I don't understand what people are saying."

"Well then, you should ask. We can explain it to you."

Frustration bubbles up inside me and threatens to boil over. Memories of the agonizing isolation in middle school flash through my mind. Shifting in my seat, I try to stay calm. "It's not that simple. I'm missing too much. I don't even know the topic. Can't I just get a book?"

On my left, Girma nudges my arm. "Saba just told us she used to call herself an Ethiopian."

My eyes widen with shock.

"Don't listen to him," she says. "I *am* Eritrean."

My curiosity craves an explanation. "I know you are Eritrean, but have you ever called yourself an Ethiopian?"

"At school, yes. Because of the war." Ethiopia claimed control of its small neighbor to the north. Eritrea did not want to be part of Ethiopia, and for thirty years Eritreans fought for independence. The war ended in 1991—two years later, the world recognized Eritrea as an independent country.

Saba continues, "Ethiopians controlled the schools. We had to speak Amharic in school. But at home, we spoke Tigrinya and called ourselves Eritreans.

"When I was a teenager we lived in Mendefera, another city in Eritrea. My father worked as a police officer and they transferred him from Asmara to Mendefera. At the high school there, I was part of a group that traveled around singing songs making fun of the Eritrean freedom fighters."

My face scrunches up in confusion. "You made fun of Eritreans fighting for freedom?"

"We had no choice," she says. "The soldiers came to the school and they forced us. They picked about twenty students from our school and told us to join the group. They gave us lyrics and forced us to learn them. We used to sing all over Eritrea, visiting different villages. One day we went to my father's village, and the people there didn't like us. They felt insulted. We were Eritreans, too. It wasn't right. But the soldiers said, 'Sing or you'll go to jail.' That's why we sang."

My voice rises with trepidation. "What happened?"

"We got fed up and told the soldiers, 'No.' We refused to sing."

One word, one thought, one daring declaration of freedom. *No*, she would not sing songs that offended her father's village. *No*, she would not serve an organization that hurt her people. *No*, she would not continue to hide her identity.

"The soldiers sent all of us to jail. The first two days, they wouldn't give us food. The soldiers would ask, 'Are you going to sing? If you don't sing, we won't give you food. You're going to stay here. You're not going to get out.' And we were hungry—so hungry! After two days we broke down and told them we would sing. They finally let us out after a week."

The injustice of throwing girls in jail for refusing to sing infuriates me. "How did you manage to go back to singing after that?"

"We sang, but in our minds, we were all making plans to become soldiers for the resistance or go to Sudan."

"Weren't you in school? Couldn't you study to become a doctor or something? Why only those two choices?"

"Because there was a war. A lot of the time we were hiding. The Ethiopians would be in the air by five a.m., flying over Mendefera dropping bombs. They did it for months—everyone would get up early and leave the city to hide in the jungles, and then come back later in the day when the bombing stopped. Sometimes we pretended we were just going out for a long picnic. Awiye cooked food for us and we would play in the trees. At the end of the day we would head home, wondering if our house was still standing.

"Even when we did make it to school, we were always thinking about the war. We weren't thinking, 'Oh, I'll study and become a doctor. I'll study and become a lawyer. I'll study and become somebody.' Our mind was only focused on the war. We had two choices: as soon as we finished high school, we could either become soldiers or go to Sudan."

"Did you consider becoming a soldier?" My voice quakes just asking the question.

"I thought about it. Almost half of my classmates joined the fighting—girls, too. But one of my friends warned me about joining. Something horrible happened to her. She wouldn't tell me exactly what happened. She kept saying, 'It's really bad, don't go.' So, me, my friend, and a cousin all decided to go to Sudan."

"Haben, eat." Grandma Awiye holds a tray of pastries out to me. She wears ankle-length floral dresses, with a long white *netsela*, a traditional headscarf. Mostly older women wear the *netselas*. No one else in our household wears one, so the headscarf is one of my clues for identifying Awiye.

"*Yekenyeley.*" *Thank you.* I reach out and feel for a pastry on the tray, the one like a sandwich with cream in the middle. Taking a bite, I savor the tantalizing cinnamon flavor. Many American treats have distinct shapes and textures that lend themselves to easy tactile identification. Eating here tends to involve a series of discoveries. Maybe in a few weeks I'll know all the foods here by touch.

I turn back to Saba. "What was it like to go to Sudan?"

Saba sips from a tiny cup of coffee, then sets it down on the table. "We weren't allowed to just leave Asmara. The Ethiopian soldiers controlled the city. If anyone wanted to leave, they needed to get permission from the Ethiopian soldiers. I was with about twenty refugees, all of us trying to escape the war. We told the soldiers we were just going to visit family in a village about twenty miles outside Asmara, so they gave us papers. We took a bus to the village, Halhale. Then at night we met up with this guy, a smuggler, who helped us get to Sudan.

"It took us three weeks. We only walked at night to hide from Ethiopian and Eritrean fighters. One night, we were walking between two hills—on one side were the Ethiopians, and on the other side were the Eritreans. They were shooting at one another. We had to duck and run for cover."

"Was the smuggler nice?"

"No!" Saba laughs. "He was incredibly mean. If anyone got tired he'd say, 'I'm going to leave you here and let the hyenas get you.' We were so tired! After the first week, my shoes fell apart and I had to walk the rest of the way barefoot. He didn't care. He still said he would leave us if we didn't keep up.

"The smuggler told us he would get a camel to carry our bags if we paid him. We'd left home carrying everything we owned on our backs, so we really wanted that camel. We gave him some money, and every night he said he would buy a camel." Saba sighs, remembering. "We never saw a camel."

"But Saba—"

"Don't say Saba, say Mommy."

My cheeks flush. "Actually, I'm too old for that."

Girma chimes in, "You should say 'Mom' and 'Dad.'"

"No, that makes me sound old!" Saba loops an arm through mine and pulls me against her. "I'm not gonna let you become a teenager."

Saba's arm tries to pin me to her side, for now and forever, while my heart pulls me toward my own trek for freedom. "Then what do you want me to call you?" I ask.

"Eh...I'm fine with Saba." Her whole body vibrates with her warm, melodic laugh. I laugh with her. Girma can't help chuckling, too.

When the laughter subsides, I urge her to continue the story. "Do you think the smuggler was telling the truth about the hyenas?"

"Oh! You know what happened?" She loosens her grip on my arm, relaxing into the sofa. "On the third night, we were walking, and all of the sudden two hyenas started circling our group. The smuggler said, 'Don't run! Stay together!' But my friend and I ran for a nearby tree. The hyenas left the group and came straight to us! Oh my god, their eyes! We flew up that tree, and the hyenas glared at us from the ground."

Her words send adrenaline racing through my veins.

"The rest of our group screamed at the hyenas and chased them away," she continues. "Another time, we crossed a river where the water rose up to my chest."

"But how did you cross the river?" I shoot Girma a questioning look, wondering if he'll crack a joke. He tries to teach her to swim when we go to the Red Sea.

"The smuggler brought ropes and we tied ourselves to them. The water scared me, but I forced myself to keep going.

"Because it was the rainy season, the region swarmed with

mosquitos. Half of us caught malaria. Actually, all of us got malaria, but some of us didn't feel the symptoms until we got to Sudan. One girl didn't make it. The guys carried her, trying to help her reach the border. Then one of the Eritrean resistance groups captured us. They wanted us to join the fighting. We told them, 'Look, we're tired, starving, and suffering from malaria. We're not in any position to fight.' They kept us for a week, then they let us go. The next night we made it to Kassala, Sudan.

"All of the Eritreans living in Kassala helped one another. One of my friends had family there, so they let me stay with them. Every Eritrean home had several refugees sleeping on the floors and in the backyards. The Sudanese people helped me get a job. I worked at a store selling clothes. After ten months, the Catholic Church brought me to the U.S. They sent me to Dallas. I hated the weather there, so I moved to the Bay Area."

In the Bay Area, Saba and Girma met through the Eritrean-Ethiopian community, a small and close-knit group. Two years later, I was born on July 29, 1988.

"I'm wondering…" My mind struggles to phrase the question just right. "How do you feel about the fact that Girma is Ethiopian?"

"He's not. He's Eritrean." She sounds annoyed.

I give Girma a quizzical look. His silence seems to invite me to press on. "No, he's not—he was born in Ethiopia."

"He's Eritrean," she insists. "His father was born in Eritrea."

"Can I speak?" Girma asks.

"Yes, you can speak," I tell him.

"I was born and raised in Ethiopia—"

"Your father is Eritrean," Saba interjects. "Therefore, you are Eritrean." She sighs. "Haben, I know what you're trying to say. I have lots of friends who are Ethiopians. The people are not the ones who caused the war. It was the government."

"Can I speak?" Girma tries again.

"Yes."

"I was born and raised in Addis Ababa, the capital of Ethiopia," he says. "I grew up there. I have feelings for that place. I still have a home there, and my sister and brother are there. At the same time, I am also Eritrean. My father was born and raised in Keren, in northern Eritrea. Every year he would take the whole family there for summer vacation. My siblings and I would hike in the mountains, swim in the lake, and chase baboons. Do I speak the language? Yes, I do. Do I have friends in Eritrea? Yes, I do. Do I empathize with the Liberation? Yes, I do. But, as I told you, I love Ethiopia, too. You can't hide this. Wherever you are born, it is a part of your life.

"How would you identify yourself, Haben? What's your nationality?"

"American." I give him a smug look, congratulating myself for the straightforward and indisputable answer.

"You are Eritrean, too," Saba corrects me. "Your parents are from Eritrea, so you are Eritrean-American."

"In that case, I'm Ethiopian, too." I'm pressing her buttons. I can't help it. Saba's relationship to Ethiopia fascinates me. She moves through the spectrum of fear to forgiveness, and I want to understand it all.

"Yes," Girma responds. "You are American, and you are Eritrean, and you are Ethiopian."

I stare at Saba, willing her to say something. I can't see her facial expressions, but I know she has an opinion.

"Your name is *Haben*!" She shouts my name like a declaration. "That's an Eritrean name!"

"It's a *Tigrinyan* name," Girma points out. "Tigrinya is also spoken in Ethiopia."

Saba waves a hand in the air. "Only in the Tigray region of Ethiopia do people speak Tigrinya. But that's not the point. *Haben* means, 'Pride!' *Haben* means, 'We stand up for our freedom.' Ethiopia had forty-eight million people. Eritrea had only three million. Ethiopia tried to crush Eritrea, but we refused to back down. And we won!" Her voice rises in jubilation. "We got our independence!"

Girma goes on, "What you have to understand, Haben, is that the Eritrean struggle was a justified one. A large neighbor tried to squash and silence a small neighbor. You don't have to be Eritrean to understand what the Eritrean people went through. Whether one is American, German, or Vietnamese, one can understand the story of a small group of people fighting for their freedom against a larger, more powerful group. What the Ethiopian government did to the Eritrean people was unjust."

"Did you know about the war when you were growing up in Addis Ababa?" I ask.

"No, I hardly knew about it. At the time, the fighting was only in Eritrea. I grew up with Ethiopian—"

"When you visited Keren, you learned about what was happening in Eritrea," Saba says.

Girma continues: "When I was in Ethiopia, the culture, the people, everything was spoken and written in Amharic. The Ethiopian government claimed Eritrea was part of Ethiopia. When my family visited Eritrea, though, it felt like a different country. Everyone spoke Tigrinya, for example. It's true that there was guerrilla warfare, but I was very young—the knowledge I had then was limited. We would go to Keren and go hiking, swimming, having fun with my friends. I didn't know about the politics. Then, when I got older, I heard about Ethiopian soldiers burning villages and hurting innocent people, and I knew that was wrong."

"How did you manage to cross the Eritrean-Ethiopian border if there was a war going on?" I wonder aloud.

"At that time, Eritrea was the fourteenth province of Ethiopia. We didn't need permission to travel to Eritrea. It was like going from California to Nevada. The fighting started in '61, but it didn't become a full-scale war until the seventies. By then I was attending college in California."

"What was school like in Ethiopia?"

"I went to St. Joseph's, a Catholic school. We had good teachers. Haile Selassie's grandkids went there, too."

Haile Selassie was the last emperor of Ethiopia. His full title reflects the mix of fear and reverence he commanded around the world: "By the Conquering Lion of the Tribe of Judah, His Imperial Majesty Haile Selassie I, King of Kings of Ethiopia, Elect of God." Haile Selassie traced his lineage to Menelik I, the son of King Solomon of ancient Israel, and Makeda, the queen of Sheba. After World War II, Haile Selassie ordered his military to prevent Eritrean self-determination. He passed away in 1975, though the war with Eritrea continued for another sixteen years.

"Haile Selassie came to the school when they opened a new building. We all gathered to hear him speak. He encouraged us to continue our education—he always supported education. He handed out degrees to the university graduates, and my sister received her degree from him. He also gave my father a medal for being an *Arbenya*."

"A what?"

"*Arbenya*. It means like a hero, a patriot. During World War II, the Italians colonized Ethiopia, Eritrea, and part of Somalia. My father was a businessman in Djibouti at the time, and on the side he helped pass on information about the Italians to Haile Selassie. What they were doing, where they stationed troops, what weapons they used, stuff like that. He was helping Haile Selassie push the Italians out. Italians prevented Eritreans and Ethiopians from going to school past the fifth grade, and forbade them from walking on the same side of the street as an Italian. Your grandfather led a group of young men in Eritrea who resisted Italian colonization. That's what we mean by *Arbenya*."

"Wow. I wish I had met Grandpa Kidane. Why didn't you stay there? Why didn't you go to college in Ethiopia?"

"Ethiopia had just one university, and only students in the top one percent of their class gained admission. I was in the top ten percent of my class—good, but not good enough. My older sister Hannah had already gone to California, so that's why my father wanted me to go to school there. He gave me two hundred dollars—that was all I had to start my life."

"He could have given you more!" Saba says. "Your father was rich." Grandpa Kidane ran a successful business producing an Ethiopian liquor called *areki.* "Why only two hundred dollars?"

"The Ethiopian government set a limit of two hundred dollars. They wanted to prevent people from moving out of the country. After I left, Ethiopia became a communist state and the government confiscated my father's properties." He pauses, remembering. "But my biggest struggle in America had nothing to do with money. In Addis, I had thirteen brothers and sisters. In San Francisco, I only had my sister Hannah, and she soon moved to Las Vegas with her boyfriend. I worked as a busboy at a burger place called Zim's, and took classes at City College. My studio in San Francisco felt like a jail cell. The loneliness almost killed me."

"Haben, do you know what happened?" Saba giggles. "His sister told me this: When he got to America, Girma couldn't cook! He didn't even know how to clean! At your grandfather's house, he had people to cook and clean for him. So, one day, your grandfather called Girma in America and asked if he should send him a housekeeper, and Girma was like, 'Yes, yes, yes!'"

I burst into hysterics. "No way! Girma, how did you manage?"

He chuckles, remembering his early mistakes. "I burned a lot of pots. I burned a lot of skillets. All while just trying to cook spaghetti and *tibs.*" *Tibs* are pieces of meat covered in Ethiopian herbs—spicy and delicious. "But really, I didn't care about food. I didn't care about money. In America, I hated the loneliness. I missed my family in Ethiopia."

*   *   *

Sitting here with these stories I can feel the similarities between their struggles with war and loss, and my struggles as a Deafblind girl in a sighted, hearing world. Saba developed the internal strength to resist an oppressive regime and survive the dangerous journey of a refugee. My father gained the courage to leave the comforts of his home—seeking independence in a strange and lonely country, practicing self-reliance over a plate of burnt spaghetti. My parents found a way through injustice, and I will, too.

Chapter Four

Gender and a Load of Bull

Asmara, Eritrea. Summer 2001.

A soul-warming sun radiates over Asmara, but my sister TT and I can't feel it. We're huddled in our grandmother's semi-dark living room, hiding.

The women in my family, including my mother, Saba, are all in the kitchen preparing food for my aunt's wedding. They plan to mince an enormous pile of onions, onions that release tear-inducing fumes. Saba told TT and me to join. We snuck off to the place in the house farthest from the kitchen.

"I'm bored!" I whine.

"I'm bored!" TT echoes. Nine-year-old TT loves animals and exploring the world, just like me. She's a few inches shorter than me, wears glasses, and is sighted and hearing. Still, our relatives frequently mix up our names. Often they just call both of us "TTHaben" or "HabenTT."

A family friend named Rimon sits across from us in an armchair. Ten years old, he's the perfect age between TT and me. He lives here in Asmara.

"Rimon, what should we do?" I ask.

"I don't know!" He sounds frustrated, too.

I fall back against the sofa and close my eyes. Whatever we do, we need to avoid the kitchen. The kitchen is a one-room building in the backyard. The large backyard has fruit trees, a chicken coop, and now for the first time this summer, a bull.

I sit up. "We could go see the bull! I mean, all the cartoons say bulls don't like the color red, so we could find out if it's true or not. It'll be like a scientific experiment! And if Saba says anything, we'll just tell her it's educational."

"Wait, what?" Rimon couldn't follow my English.

I stand up and point to the other side of the room. "*Over there, bull*," I say, in my best broken Tigrinya. I point to where I am standing, "*Me, here*." I grab a sweater off the couch and wave it energetically. "*Toro! Toro!*"

"Aha! Yes!" Rimon leaps out of his chair.

"Wait! We need something red!" I point to the sweater. "*Keih*." Red.

"Oh, okay. Where can we find red?" he asks.

"Follow me!" I race out into the hall, moving with memory and residual vision. I turn left into our bedroom. The house has three bedrooms, and my parents, TT, and I share one of them.

Once inside, I open our suitcase. Every item has a different texture, a different shape, a different style. My hands search through the clothes, and finally I pull out a top that meets our color requirements.

"That's my shirt!" TT says.

Technically it's mine—it just doesn't fit me anymore. "We're only going to hold it. It'll be fine."

TT crosses her arms, a begrudging concession.

I lead the way out of the bedroom, across the hall, and into a second bedroom. This one has a window overlooking the part of the backyard where the bull awaits his fate. Leaning over the windowsill, I squint at the dark colors below.

"Can you see it?" I ask.

"Yes." TT has her keep-me-out-of-this voice. I immediately know it would be pointless to ask for descriptions like, how big is it? How long are the horns? Has it spotted us? But maybe she'll answer this one:

"He's tied up, right?"

TT ignores me.

I turn to Rimon. "Is he tied up?"

"Yeah, he's tied," says Rimon. "So, are you going to do it?" Beneath his question I hear another one: *Are you brave enough to try?*

The challenge urges me on, flooding courage into my arms. I hang the red shirt out the window, shake it, and run back inside.

Nothing happens.

I try it again, this time holding it out longer, vigorously waving the red shirt.

Nothing happens.

"We have to go outside," I tell Rimon and TT.

"No!" TT blocks the door. "You can't, it's not safe!"

"TT, don't worry," I assure her. "He's tied up. He can't do anything."

"Yes he can! We're gonna get killed!"

Her fear stirs up mine. Are his horns that long? What has she seen? What if I misjudge the length of the ropes and get too close?

My desire to explore the world outweighs my doubts. "TT, how about this: you stay in here and watch us through the window. If anything happens, you can be the hero and call for help. Rimon and I will go outside, but we'll be careful. I promise."

TT stands there, blocking the door.

"TT, please," Rimon says.

Still not speaking, she stomps away from the door.

Rimon and I skid to a stop at the corner of the house just before the bull's part of the backyard. Stepping around that corner will bring us within feet of the animal.

I shove the red shirt into Rimon's arms. "Here, you first!"

"Hey!" He pushes the shirt back at me. "No, you first!"

I try to give it back to him, but he stays well out of my reach. I suddenly realize that TT can hear us through the window. She deserves a fearless sister, a role model.

Summoning my courage, I take two steps forward. Somewhere in the space in front of me is a big bad bull. Adrenaline pumps through my veins as I realize I don't know the exact location of the animal. My feet feel for any vibrations from its movement. Nothing. Since I can't see or hear the bull, I need the next best thing: feeling the ground shake when the bull roars.

I raise the red shirt in front of me and shake it, waving it to the left, to the right, to the front...

"He's not doing anything!" I complain to Rimon.

Rimon snatches the red shirt and takes my place in front of the bull. "*Toro!*" He jumps up and down waving the red shirt in the air. "*Toro! Toro! Toro!*" All the jumping looks like a wild dance. A piss-off-the-beast dance. A guaranteed-to-get-a-response dance.

"RIMON!" a woman yells.

At that exact moment, I remember that people in the kitchen have a clear view of the bull. *Oops.*

Rimon and I run back into the living room where TT meets us. Laughing, we recount the adventure to one another, comparing all three perspectives. Rimon earns top marks for his daring performance. I win points for my brilliant idea. TT admits it wasn't a bad idea. After all, we managed to avoid cooking!

Preparations for the wedding intensify over the next two days. My backyard has transformed into an obstacle course of wine barrels and construction materials. Worst of all, the backyard smells atrocious after the bull's slaughter. I no longer walk through the backyard alone for fear of stepping in something disgusting or walking into hanging bull parts.

The bedroom feels safe. No dead animals dripping blood. No invisible wires trying to trip me up. No exasperated relatives wondering why I don't recognize them. In here, I can relax.

Someone opens the bedroom door.

Placing a bookmark in my braille book, I brace myself for a conversation.

The person walks over to the closet and starts searching through it. She's wearing a *netsela*, a traditional white scarf that covers the wearer's hair and upper body. Usually only Grandma Awiye wears the *netsela* around the house, but right now all the adult women wear them out of respect for the visiting elders. With all of the women covered in white and all of them being practically the same height, I can't tell them apart. So I wait for a clue.

The woman closes the closet door and walks over to me. "What are you doing in here? You need to help us prepare!" It's Saba.

"I will! As soon as I finish this chapter."

"No, now. TT is cooking with us. Rimon is helping us set up the tent. Everybody's asking me, 'Where is Haben? Where is Haben?' Everybody is working except you. Why are you refusing to help?"

My face grows hot. Explaining my discomfort with all the obstacles out there feels impossible. "What do you want me to do?"

"Come help us in the kitchen."

"No, I don't want to become a Cinderella."

Saba laughs, a happy, musical sound. "What does that even mean?"

"Look at Hiwet." I name her youngest sister. "She spends almost all day cooking and cleaning like Cinderella. She hardly has a social life, and that's not fair."

"No, it's not fair. But if everyone here helps with the work, then it won't all be on Hiwet. See, *that's* why we need you in the kitchen."

"But that's how it starts! Once a girl goes to work in the kitchen, she'll always work in the kitchen. Everybody will start asking her to 'cook this, clean that, make this, bring that.' If she ever asks for someone else to do a chore people just say, 'Oh, but you're so much better at it than me.' I don't want to become a Cinderella."

"Then what are you going to do?"

"I'm not opposed to doing chores, I just don't want to do work that's designated as girls' work. What's Teme doing?" I ask after her youngest brother.

"Okay, let's go find Teme." She heads for the door and I follow close behind.

Chaos greets us in the hallway. Loud animated voices come from the living room. We walk past it, stepping out into the backyard. Somewhere to our right is the doghouse and its occupant, a white spotted mutt named Hyatt. We go out the front gate to the unpaved street in front of the compound. The temperature drops from hot to warm as we step under a huge tent that blocks out the sun.

Saba stops in front of a group sitting around a table. "Teme, Haben wants to help you."

"Wait…" I sniff the air, trying to identify the odd smell. "What are they doing?"

"They're cutting meat for the stew," she says.

My jaw drops. How can she do this after my stellar Cinderella speech?

"Go sit down on the other side. Jessica is here, too." Saba knows I love Jessica. My twenty-year-old cousin has entertained me with stories of college life in the Netherlands.

Squeezing onto a bench at the table, I look around. There are about eight people at this table, guys to the left and right of me. I don't know which one is Teme, but across from me and to the left is a lighter-skinned person who must be Jessica. Every now and then someone reaches into a big pile in the middle. I touch the pile and discover sticky, hand-sized chunks of meat. A piece coats my palm with the sticky liquid as I transfer it to the cutting board in front of me.

The guy to my right passes me a knife with a long and wide blade.

"Here." Saba puts a tiny piece of meat in my hand. "Make it that small, Cinderella."

"Don't call me Cinderella." My cheeks burn as I sense everyone at the table staring at me, wondering why Saba called me Cinderella. They wouldn't dare. If one of them calls me that name...

I position the chunk of meat in front of me so the shorter side faces perpendicular to my knife. My fingers estimate a small section to chop off.

How rude of these boys to not identify themselves. They should say hi.

My right hand positions the knife just past the fingers on my left hand. I start sawing the meat, putting weight into my right hand. The blade suddenly connects with the cutting board, which means it's gone all the way through the meat. I scrape the cut piece aside with the blade, clearing space for the next one. With my left hand, I estimate another section and reposition the knife.

This must be the big bad bull.

Slicing all the way through, I push this small piece to the side.

Remember how you humiliated me, bull? *Remember?*

Finding a rhythm, my fingers start to move faster. I cut piece after piece, building a little pile.

You learned things the hard way—ignoring me was a deadly mistake!

Sawing furiously, I finish the last piece.

While I work, the guys talk around me. Mumble, mumble. Fine, be that way. Don't include me in your conversations.

I snatch another chunk of meat from the large pile and start cutting again.

The group bursts into laughter. Murmurs. Muttering. More laughter.

I keep my head down while I work. I hate missing out. I hate exclusion. I *hate* cooking.

I pull a new chunk of meat from the big pile.

"Eww!" Jessica bolts from the table.

Looking around, I try to figure out why she left. No one says anything, and no one else leaves. Shrugging, I go back to work. My left hand positions the new chunk of meat while my right hand holds the knife.

What on earth? Carefully putting down the knife, I examine the meat with both hands. The squishy flesh has a round base and a long shaft.

My pulse skyrockets. It's the bull's penis!

My heart hammers in my chest as I fight the urge to run. Stay calm. The guys are definitely staring. They probably set this up as a joke, expecting the girls to flee shrieking.

A steely calm washes over me as I resolve to stay. I absolutely can sit here and cut meat. Go ahead, boys—watch me!

Gripping the knife with my right hand, I once again use my left hand to position the meat.

This one's for Cinderella!

I begin sawing the meat, and it wiggles and squirms under the knife. I press down on the blade, sawing with even more force.

A large hand slips under mine and rescues the organ. A triumphant smirk lights up my face as I watch the guy walk away toward the backyard. There, that'll teach them to stop pulling pranks.

Was that really the bull's...? My mind skims through memories from my seventh-grade sex-ed class. Maybe, possibly. Oh. My. God.

My stomach churns with revulsion. I can't sit here anymore. I'm done. If Saba asks why I'm not cooking, I'll just tell her the story. I'd love to help, Mom, but I had a horrifying encounter with a bull penis.

I put my knife down and head back to the house, stepping cautiously through the obstacle course of wedding preparations.

Not knowing the names of the family members around me, even after working closely with them, fills me with an aching loneliness. I could have asked them to identify themselves. I could have asked Jessica to explain what was going on. By focusing all my energy on proving my fearlessness, framing the situation as me-against-them, I perpetuated and guaranteed my own exclusion.

Chapter Five

Key by Key

Asmara, Eritrea. Summer 2001.

A rocky, unpaved road winds in front of my grandmother's house. Tall brick and metal gates line the street, marking our neighbors' yards. Last week, my aunt's wedding tent stood on this street. People danced and cheered, drank and ate, partying for three whole days. Now the street feels empty. Cars roll by slowly, mindful of the kids who treat the road as a playground for soccer, marbles, and tag. I stroll down the street, trailing the side to stay out of the way.

A hand grabs my arm. Cold fear slices through me like a knife. The hand belongs to a kid three inches shorter than me.

"What?" I breathe, telling myself to calm down. He could be a cousin, or a family friend.

He shouts something. The jarring sound sends my pulse racing.

"What?" I ask in Tigrinya.

More shouting.

I jerk my arm free. He grabs my wrist with both hands. His shrieks sound desperate. I twist my wrist, but his strong grip just tightens around my arm. That's when I see a group of ten kids gathered around us. The other kids start shouting, too.

My fists clench. I ground myself, preparing to kick. The Oakland Unified School District's blindness program provided us with self-defense training. Memories from the lesson flash through my mind.

A girl steps forward and wraps her hands around my other wrist. Her grip is gentle, light, meant to touch rather than restrain. "It's Lydia. Can you bring the keyboard? Please?"

I stare at her, perplexed. "Keyboard?" My grandmother's house doesn't have a computer. I rack my brain for possible meanings. "Do you mean the toy piano? *Musica?*"

"Yes." Lydia waves my arm side to side. "Please! Please!"

The shouting of the kids behind her morphs into a chorus of, "Please! Please!"

"Sure." My shoulders relax.

Shouting always scares me. I can't hear the nuances that distinguish happy cheering from furious swearing. Often, people shout at me thinking I'll hear them better. It just makes me want to run away, or kick them.

I pull my left arm back, out of the stranger's grasp. A lot of kids don't know that a strong grip signals aggression. Most kids tend to ignore tactile communication. I keep reminding myself to pause and check before reacting.

Lydia holds my hand and we walk with our arms swinging. She's eleven, a year younger than me. She speaks the best

English of all the neighborhood kids, so the others often ask her to explain games to TT and me.

The group gathers at my grandmother's front door. I wave at them as I go through.

Music and I have a complicated relationship. My limited hearing means I miss most of the music around me. Part of the sounds produced by keyboards fall within the small range of hearing I have in the high frequencies. My ears can process certain types of simple, straightforward melodies—the less noise the better.

Engaging with music through my sense of touch heightened my understanding of sound. In school, Ms. Scott taught me braille music. Each musical note has a corresponding braille symbol. After memorizing the braille music for "Are You Sleeping Brother John," I then proceeded to the large keyboard in our classroom and played the song. The challenge of training my fingers to perform the pattern pleased me.

When Ms. Scott introduced chords, my progress petered out. The low frequencies of the chords drowned out the high frequency sounds in the melody. The whole left half of the keyboard sounded dull, like the rumblings of a washing machine. Music will never fill my soul with joy the way it seems to for the people around me.

My family adores the toy piano. We brought it from the United States for my little cousin. He banged on it a few times, then abandoned it. My twenty-four-year-old uncle Abraham picked up the purple children's toy and began playing Eritrean songs by ear. His ability to identify a note just by listening to it astounded me. Key by key, Abraham taught me how to play the music of Eritrea.

When I emerge outside bearing the precious toy, the crowd of kids at the gate has grown. Lydia takes my arm and leads me to a pair of large rocks where we sit down. The crowd follows, forming a semicircle around us.

I proffer the keyboard to her, and she begins to play a melody. At the end of her piece, the group applauds.

Lydia passes the keyboard to a new girl, who takes her place on the rock.

"What is your name?" I ask.

"Sara."

Smiling, I wave at the keyboard. Holding the toy with one hand, she pecks at keys with the other. The notes sound disconnected. She starts over, and this time I catch parts of the song she's trying to play. She stops and starts again.

I reach over and play the first seven notes of the song. My index finger taps out the pattern again, going slowly to help her memorize the sequence. The other kids lean in to watch.

I turn the keyboard back to Sara. She hits a few wrong notes, but quickly corrects herself. On her fourth try, she plays the pattern all the way through without mistakes.

"Awesome!" I give her two thumbs up.

While I'm teaching Sara, the kids are teaching me something, too. I've wondered what I could offer a sighted, hearing world, a world where it feels like I'm always the last one to know something. Society frames people with disabilities as incapable of contributing. And yet, these kids treat me like someone with gifts to share and lessons to teach.

Sara returns the keyboard to me. I play the next seven notes in the song, repeat them, then pass the keyboard back to her.

Sara plays, then leaps off the rock. The kids start shouting. My heart slams against my rib cage as I squint at the crowd, trying to spot the source of the distress.

Beside me, a tall lanky man sits down on the rock with my keyboard in his lap. He starts playing a song.

I power on my sternest, iciest, most authoritative voice. "We're taking turns here. Give the keyboard back to Sara."

"Haben, don't you know me? It's Tomas." He's a nineteen-year-old who lives two houses down.

My frown deepens. "Tomas, you need to get in line. It's not your turn. Give it back to Sara."

"Okay, okay." Tomas mutters something in Tigrinya. "Just one more song."

My stomach twists into knots. I don't want him to play even one song, but I can't make him return the keyboard to the kids. "Okay, one song."

He starts to play. The music taunts me, mocking my inability to control what happens to me or the treasured keyboard. It feels like an even stronger force has grabbed and twisted my wrists, leaving me helpless.

At the end of his piece, Tomas finally hands the keyboard to me. "Bye, Haben."

I glare at him. "Bye."

The next day, I head outside again for a walk. My family can sometimes hear the front door open and close, so my hands work slowly, carefully, quietly as I slide the bolt out of its lock.

I pull the door open just wide enough for me to slip through and...*bam*! A pair of hands shove me forward. I spin around. One of my little cousins pushes past me.

I catch his arm. "Did your mom say you could go out?"

"Leave me alone!" Only one of the little cousins speaks English: Yafet. He was born and raised in California, like me.

"Let's go ask your mom if—"

Yafet yanks his arm free and runs.

I chase after him on a road teeming with rocks and potholes. I move at a fast walk, my toes slightly raised to maintain my balance whenever my shoes smash into things. Taking long strides, I finally close the gap between us, catching part of his shirt. "Yafet, stop!"

"Let go!" He wiggles free, running farther down the street.

"I'm gonna tell your mom!" I shout, hustling after the wild child.

Yafet suddenly veers right. I change course, following. He veers left. I veer left, too. He runs right, then left again. He runs up to a gate and disappears.

That's where Tomas lives! My heart starts pounding with panic. My baby cousin has entered the wolf's den!

Taking a deep breath, I stride over to the gate. A person stands in front of the door.

"Hi, did Yafet go inside?" I ask.

"Baaaaaaaa! Baaa!"

I roll my eyes. "Fabio?" Tomas has a fifteen-year-old brother who likes to joke around.

"Baaaaaa! Baaaaa! Baaaaaaaaaaaaa!" he bleats.

44

The corners of my lips curl up in a smile. "All right, Black Sheep. Have you any wool?"

"Baa! Baaaa!"

"Excellent. I'm gonna go get the bag of wool and the little boy." I push the gate open and walk inside.

A rectangular courtyard stretches out before me, with a wall on my left and a building to my right. I walk forward cautiously. A closed door appears on the right. Yafet could be in there. Or not. I keep walking, venturing deeper into the courtyard.

Someone approaches. "Hi, Haben!"

"Hi." I offer the woman my hand. She takes it, then gives me a kiss on each cheek. "What's your name?"

"Soliana. I am Tomas's sister."

"Nice to meet you. Is Yafet here?"

"Yes. I'll show you." Soliana takes my hand and guides me through a door. A television plays along the left wall. Two people sit on a sofa by the television. A small, Yafet-sized person lounges in an armchair in front of me.

"Haben! It's Tomas."

I do a double take. Most people don't identify themselves. "Hi…"

"Come in! Come sit!" Tomas projects his voice. I'm surprised that I can hear him across the room. He mastered the art of projecting without vocal tension.

I walk around the two armchairs to reach the sofa. There's no room on the sofa, so I sit down on the bed next to it.

Tomas leans forward in his seat. "How's your family?"

"They're good."

"How's Mussie?"

My eyebrows shoot up in surprise. Tomas knows my brother.

Family history never fits into a single, neat narrative, especially in a large family spread across four continents. The stories unfold over years, detail by detail, person by person. Somehow, someway, Tomas holds a part of my family history.

My two brothers mostly grew up separate from me. American culture might label them as half-brothers. In Eritrea we just say brothers. The oldest, twelve years my senior, is Awet. He teaches kids at a school in California. The other brother, six years my senior, is Mussie. He is the only other person in my family who is Deafblind.

Tomas's question triggers memories of family conversations. Mussie grew up here, with Grandma Awiye. Is that how Tomas knows him? Grandma tried to provide Mussie with an education, but the schools said they could not teach a Deafblind child. Mussie stayed at home while the other kids attended school. After several frustrating years, Mussie immigrated to the United States. He finally gained access to school at age twelve.

I swallow, trying to clear the lump in my throat. "Mussie is doing well. He's in New York at the Helen Keller National Center. He's staying there for nine months to learn independence skills. They work on traveling with a white cane, using assistive technology, braille, sign language, cleaning, cooking...Can you cook?"

"A little bit."

"Uh huh. I bet Mussie cooks more than you."

Tomas talks to the person next to him on the sofa. They chat for a bit. "Haben, this is Dawit. Do you know Dawit? He's my friend."

"Nice to meet you." We shake hands.

"So Mussie is okay?" Tomas continues.

"Yes. He graduated from high school and now he is getting training in New York. Why?"

"We used to hang out all the time. We were best friends. We were like this. You know this?"

"This?"

Tomas shows me his hand. His middle and index finger are twisted together.

Laughing, I nod. "You were very close."

"Yes! We were very close. We did everything together. I wanted to know that he's doing okay. Tell him we miss him and that he should come visit us."

"I will."

Soliana asks something from the doorway.

"Haben, do you want tea?" Tomas repeats the question for me.

"Sure."

Soliana hands me a cup of tea. Her kindness touches me. Then a new thought surprises me: the guy who jostled his way into the center of a group of kids and snatched a toy from a little girl actually has a warm side.

Sighted, hearing people can process multiple social details at a glance, details like facial expressions, body language, spoken words, and vocal inflection. For a Deafblind person, the world presents environmental information piece-by-piece. Each new piece of information has the potential to flip the feel of a situation.

I place the empty tea cup on the table. "I'm going to go home and let everyone know that Yafet is here. Thank you for the tea."

Someone speaks from the doorway.

Tomas responds in Tigrinya, then he turns to me. "Fabio wants to ask you something."

Fabio bounces the bed as he plops down next to me. "Baaaaa! Baaaaaa!"

Rapid-fire Tigrinya from Tomas.

My eyes sparkle with laughter. "Hi, Black Sheep! Where's that bag of wool you promised the little boy?"

"What? What do you mean?" Fabio asks.

"There's a song in America called 'Baa Baa Black Sheep,' so I named you Black Sheep because you sound like one."

"Ah, okay... I was wondering, can you get your keyboard?"

I burst into incredulous laughter. "You, too? Okay, I'll go get it."

Chapter Six

Dancing in Enchanted Hills

Napa, California. Summer 2003.

"Haben, this is your last chance," a British voice warns.

The blind high school students attending Enchanted Hills Camp can all identify the British counselors by their voices, except me. I just turned fifteen, and camp is the first big adventure of my fifteenth year. The camp offers swimming, boating, horseback riding, craft-making, hiking, sports, and theater.

Blind and sighted counselors teach blind campers how to do all of these activities, from safely mounting a horse to playing goalball. In goalball, players roll a basketball-sized ball with bells in it, sending it at top speed across the court. The opposing team members throw themselves on the floor in the ball's path, blocking it from entering the goal zone. All the players, sighted or blind, wear sleepshades (eye masks) to even the playing field. Goalball is a popular sport here, but I quickly discovered that my limited hearing makes it difficult for me to determine the ball's path of travel. So I'm avoiding goalball this year.

This year, I want to try theater.

"Haben? Don't you want to audition?" The British counselor asks. I've missed half of what they've said during the audition. As far as I can tell, people have been singing songs to audition for parts in *West Side Story*. Twelve blind campers sit in chairs facing the stage.

Heart racing, I shake my head no.

"Come on, give it a try."

Sinking into my seat, I shake my head again.

"Okay. We're done here, everyone can go. We'll do announcements after lunch."

The sounds of chairs scraping against the floor echo around the large room. Tap, tap, tap. Some campers use white canes to find their way to the door. I have a white cane, too. It's leaning against the wall of my closet at home. The cane helps me navigate unfamiliar places. I don't need it at camp because I've learned the lay of the land. My residual vision helps, too. I can see the white walls, the sunlight pouring in through the open front door, and the six people walking in front of me.

Outside, I step away from the group. The summer sun warms my skin. A light breeze carries the smell of horses from the stables down the road. A long, paved road runs from the cabins all the way up to the dining hall. The road has a three-foot-high rope along each side. Some campers like holding the rope to help them stay oriented. Other campers use their canes or residual vision.

Walking along the left edge of the road, I start looking for the horses. There's one! Oh, and someone else is here.

"Hey, it's Robin," she says.

Last year, Robin and I bonded over our shared sense of humor. We performed a skit together at the camp talent show. She goes to the California School for the Blind, and I attend Skyline, a mainstream public high school in Oakland. We only see each other at camp.

"Hi! It's Haben." I notice she's holding her hand out to the horse. "What are you feeding them?"

"Apples. Want one?" She hands me an apple.

I spot another horse, one with a chestnut coat and black mane. Standing next to Robin, I hold the apple out to the horse. As it chews, I raise my free hand to its head. Gently, I stroke the warm hair along its face, marveling at the size of its head. My hand rests on the horse's cheek, just feeling the movement as it chews.

The horse takes another bite, and its mouth grazes the palm of my hand. "Don't bite my fingers, please."

Robin cackles. "You sound so serious! Like saying that would actually make a difference!"

"It does. If you tell the world something, the world will hear it. You should tell your horse not to bite you, too."

"Don't..." Robin starts giggling. She takes a deep breath and faces her horse. "Don't...Don't bite me!" She doubles over laughing. "This is silly! I can't believe you made me say that. Let's change the subject. What did you do this morning?"

"I went to the auditions." My hand strokes the horse's cheek.

"Nice! What part did you get?"

My heart skips a beat. "Nothing."

"What! Why?"

"Because…" I lower my voice. "They wanted someone who could sing. I can't sing."

"Of course you can sing. Anyone can sing."

"No. I seriously can't sing. I can't tell if something is off-key. It's a hearing thing."

"Oh."

A tight ball of sadness settles in my chest. Even blind camp leaves me feeling excluded. They expect people to hear the ball for goalball. They expect people to hear the music for the play. All day long it's listen to this, listen to that.

"Hey," Robin pipes up. "We should do a skit for the talent show again!"

"Sure."

Two people approach us. "You girls are in trouble now," the tall one says. "We've caught you horsing around."

"Oh, please!" Robin crosses her arms. "And who are you supposed to be?"

"I'm Greg."

"I'm Robin, and this is Haben."

"Get out of here! You made that up!"

Robin laughs. "Those really are our names!"

"Fine, then," he says. "I'm Blair, and this is Claire."

"We're not making it up! My name really is Robin, and my friend really is Haben."

Wait a minute. If Greg thinks Robin rhymes with Haben, then is Robin mispronouncing my name? Is she saying, "Habin?" Or maybe Greg means Haben and Robin rhyme in a loose, Dr. Seuss way. I can't hear these auditory nuances. This is exactly why I don't sing.

"Okay, okay. If you say so," Greg says. "I wanted to tell you girls that there's a dance class that's about to start. You two should come."

Robin turns to me. "Haben?"

"I...I'm not sure. I'm not any good at dancing."

"This will be a great opportunity to learn," he says. "A blind woman who's a professional dancer will be teaching salsa."

"A blind dance teacher?" My eyes widen in astonishment.

"She studied salsa in Cuba and also trained in Spain."

I must have misheard. "Did you say a *blind* dancer?"

"Yes, she's blind."

A thousand questions whir through my mind, each one vying for attention. "How did she learn? How does she teach if she's blind?"

"Why don't you go take the class and find out?"

"Okay."

My spirits drop as we enter the Kiva, the site of the awful auditions. About ten people stand around chatting. Robin and I walk over to the front. A tall woman and man are talking quietly near the "stage" area.

"So," Robin says. "Do you dance at home?"

"Not really. My family does these Eritrean dances where everyone travels in a large circle. Every time I try, my mom goes, 'Haben, move your shoulders!' Every time I try, I get something wrong. 'Ha-ben, move your shoulders more.' 'Ha-ben, move your shoulders faster.'"

"That sounds hard."

"When I want to stop she gets so disappointed. 'Ha-ben, I want you to dance with me.' 'Ha-ben, we want you with us.'"

"Your mom says your name a lot."

"Yeah..." Now Robin definitely knows how to pronounce my name.

The instructor calls from the front. "Hello, EHC!"

"EHC's the place to be!" Everyone shouts and claps.

"My name is Denise Vancil. I'm going to be teaching you all salsa today. First, I'll tell you a little bit about my background. I've been dancing pretty much all my life. I started with tap dancing. Then I picked up other dances—jazz, modern, swing, salsa, merengue, flamenco. I love dancing and I've traveled all over the world to learn these dances. Over the next few days, we're going to focus on salsa, merengue, and swing, so we can get you ready for *West Side Story*. How many of you auditioned for the play?"

Silence.

"Some of you may not know that I'm blind," Denise says. "I can't see if anyone is raising their hand. I need you to use your voices. If you auditioned for the play, say 'me.'"

Several people call out.

"Great!" Denise continues. "I've been totally blind for most of my life, since I was thirteen. I'm telling you this because I want you to know that you don't need to see to be able to dance. If anyone has told you that you can't dance, they're wrong. You don't need to see to teach dance, either."

Standing in the front row, I listen with all my might. Learning from a confident blind woman is a novelty. I want to capture her every word, study her every movement, and memorize her every lesson.

"Okay, let's get started. I want everyone to face me. Face the direction of my voice. Those of you who can see a little bit, feel free to come up to the front. Get as close as you want."

Delighted, I immediately step forward, positioning myself three feet in front of Denise. Robin and five other people also step forward.

"We're going to start off with your feet together, facing forward. Okay, now move your feet about six inches apart. Your feet should still be directly under you. Each foot should be directly beneath each shoulder. How are we doing? Any questions?"

Someone asks a question.

"Let me check. I'll come over and look." Denise walks over to the speaker.

So far, this lesson's a breeze.

Denise walks back to the front. "So, this is our starting position. I want you all to remember this. Next, I want everyone to step forward with your left foot. Just a small step."

Watching Denise's feet, I copy her movements. She's only one person over to my left, so I can still see her feet.

"When you make that step, transfer your weight onto it. Most of your weight should be on your left foot. Not all of it. You'll still have a little weight on your right foot, but most of it will be on your left foot. Got it? Great. This is 'one.' This is the first basic step. For 'two,' you're going to step in place with your right foot and transfer weight to it. Did everybody do two?"

Kids start giggling. Confused, I recall the last thing Denise said. Oh, *do two* sounds like *do number two*. I roll my eyes.

"Let's keep going," Denise says. "Remember, I'll check in with everyone one-on-one, too. So, for 'three,' take your left foot and bring it back to the starting position. Let's go through that again. 'One,' step forward with your left foot. 'Two,' step in place with your right foot. 'Three,' bring your left foot back to the starting position. I want everyone to keep practicing that. One, two, three. One, two, three. I'm going to go around and check in with each of you. Keep practicing."

Denise steps forward to Robin. They talk quietly, and I stop practicing so I can watch. Denise steps behind Robin and puts her hands on Robin's waist as Robin does the steps. Denise talks to Robin some more, and then moves in my direction.

"Hi!" I step closer to better hear her. "My name is Haben."

"Haben?"

Uh oh. I'm not sure how she's pronouncing it. "Yes, Haben."

"Nice to meet you, Haben," Denise says. "Would it be okay if I feel you doing the steps?"

"Sure!"

Denise steps behind me and puts her hands on my waist. She maintains a light touch as I do the three steps.

"Great! Keep practicing." She then proceeds to the next person.

A huge smile spreads across my face. Of course a blind person can teach salsa. She can feel footwork through the waist, the hands, the shoulders...The whole body is connected. People who train themselves to listen to the body develop tactile intelligence.

After touching base with everyone, Denise returns to the front and teaches us the rest of the basic step. "Okay, now I want everyone to partner up," she says. "Find a partner. Talk to each other. Go!"

Robin walks off toward someone. I wonder if she spotted her crush. Brave Robin!

I look around hoping to see someone who needs a partner. Blurry figures float around the room.

A tall guy with dark glasses appears in front of me. My heart drops to the floor, rolls down the hill, and locks the door of the girls' cabin.

Steve doesn't see the alarm on my face. "Need a partner?" he asks.

I hesitate. "For the dance."

"How about for life?"

"No."

"What? Come on! Give me a chance!"

Denise calls, "Does everyone have a partner?"

Steve puts his hands out to me, palms up.

I turn to the front, facing Denise.

"Okay, now I want you to hold hands," Denise instructs.

"Yeah!" Steve cheers.

Stifling a laugh, I put my hands in his. He lifts our hands above our heads and launches into a booty-shaking, hands-waving, silent, ecstatic dance.

A surprised giggle escapes my mouth. I pull his hands down. Thankfully, Steve stops dancing.

"On the count of three," says Denise, "I want you to do the basic step with your partner. Remember, ladies start by stepping forward with the left foot. Guys start by stepping back on the right foot. We're going to turn on the music now. Music, please!"

Music begins playing. It sounds festive and lively. I can hear the high frequency parts of the music, but not the beat.

Then I notice the beat flowing through Steve's hands. His arms, his feet, his shoulders, his whole body transmits the rhythm. My hands sense all of this as we dance. I can't hear the beat, but I can feel it. Tactile intelligence.

Denise comes over and puts one hand on Steve's wrist and one hand on my wrist. She stands there observing our dance, then turns to me and begins speaking.

"I can't hear you over the music," I tell her.

She gently takes my hands and puts them on her waist. She goes through the basic steps, emphasizing each move. Her core sways side to side with each step. Left, right, left. Right, left, right. Denise then guides my hands to her feet. Crouching on the floor, I follow her feet with my hands as she goes through the basic step. Oh, she steps out on the balls of her feet, keeping her heels up. My eyes had missed that detail.

Denise stops dancing and I stand up. She moves behind me and places her hands on my waist. Cautiously, I shift my weight to the left and step forward on the ball of my left foot. Mindful of her hands, I start each step by moving my core. One, two, three, hold; five, six, seven. Her hands remain on my waist, so I run through it again. One, two, three, hold; five, six, seven.

She pats my shoulder and shouts something.

"Thank you!" I yell over the music.

Denise soon has the whole room performing turns, and Steve and I execute them flawlessly. He's a great dancer, actually. His movements feel graceful. When he improvises moves, I glide along with the flow of our rhythm. Every movement has a natural opposite, and I seem to instinctively understand all of his hand signals. Tactile intelligence.

How amazing to understand without straining to see, to just know without straining to hear. Salsa dancing requires me to utilize my strongest ability: feeling.

Dancing, spinning, I revel in the smooth flow of our movements.

The music fades. Steve lifts my hand and plants a kiss.

"Hey!" I snatch my hand away. "I didn't say you could do that!"

"Oh!" Steve wails. He steps back, clutching at his chest. "You just stuck a dagger through my heart!"

The kids around us titter. Part of me wants to laugh, too. Yet part of me wants him kicked out of camp. Just when I started feeling comfortable following his hands, he shatters my trust in one fell swoop.

"Okay!" Denise calls for our attention. "That's it for our class. You all did really great. I'm going to be here for the next few days, so you'll have more opportunities to learn more dances. Now it's time to head up to lunch."

Walking outside, Steve falls into step beside me. "I've been dancing all my life," he says. "I've danced with a lot of people. You're a really good dancer, you know that?"

"Mhm." I take long strides up the path to the dining hall.

Steve keeps up. "I mean it. You're really good. We should dance together at the dance party. We'll be the best dancers in all of Napa."

I shake my head. "No way. I haven't forgotten what you just did."

"What the...are you serious? All I did was kiss your hand!"

My lips curl up in a smile. "I trusted you to lead the dance. Kissing my hand was not part of the dance."

"Jesus! You're being ridiculous." Steve waves his hands in the air as he searches for a response. "Kissing someone's hand is a sign of respect. It's a polite thing to do. It's not romantic at all."

I bite my lip to keep from laughing. I don't know if his vision allows him to see facial expressions. I hope he can't see I'm laughing! Finally, the laughter passes, allowing me to make my voice serious. "You didn't kiss Denise's hand."

"You want me to kiss her hand? If you'll dance with me, I'll kiss her hand! I'll do it!"

"No."

Steve leaps forward, pulls the dining hall door open, and gestures for me to enter first. My pace quickens as I glide past him and the memory of our dance together.

He catches up to me. "Are you really saying I can't dance with you at the dance party?"

"Yes."

"What? This isn't fair! I've never met a girl so—"

Turning away, I speed walk to the one place he can't go: the ladies' room.

Dancing salsa felt glorious. The connection two people share during a dance carries a special joy grounded in presence. Now if only I could find a way to dance salsa without boys...

Chapter Seven

Dishing Up Trouble

Oakland, California. Fall 2003.

One evening after school, I sit in my room holding a piece of paper. Skyline High School has a club called buildOn, where students learn to make a positive impact both in our local community and abroad. Next spring, buildOn will send a group of students to Mali, West Africa, to build a school. My application for the trip needs one last thing: my parents' signature.

Given my parents' protectiveness, this calls for a strategy.

I hop off my bed. Three short steps bring me to the door. I walk down the carpeted hallway, my whole body listening for any signs of my parents—vibrations through the floor, moving shapes in my limited field of vision, or a telltale noise. Then, in the distance, I hear the incoherent spluttering of the television.

I run for the living room.

My mom, Saba, keeps the dining room organized, with chairs tucked into their place. The only obstacle is a step going up from the dining room to the living room. Because the dining room and living room have an off-white wall-to-wall carpet, a lot of people trip over the step. They can't see it. I can't see it, either. So, when I near the approximate area of the step, I jump.

Next to me, the glowing television spews out noise. Two dark leather couches face the TV. I clasp my hands in front of me and stare at the couches.

No response.

Come on, I know you're there.

I stand waiting. And waiting. And waiting.

Maybe they're not here. Just because a TV is on doesn't mean someone's watching.

I step in front of the TV.

"Yes?" Saba calls from the couch.

"I just want you to know that I'm going to do the dishes."

"Thank you, honey."

I hop over the invisible step, cross through the dining room, and turn left into the kitchen. I feel around the rim of the sink for a sponge. My hand finds one on the top right corner of the sink; my other hand picks up the tall and curvy bottle of soap. I tilt the bottle so that the nozzle touches the sponge. Positioned, I squeeze. My thumb on the sponge measures the amount of soap pouring out.

Warm water runs through my hands. I lower a hand into the sink, then sigh. The sink has a lot of dishes. I run the soapy sponge over a plate, my fingers perusing both sides for any stubborn bits of food. Finding none, I rinse the plate in the stream of water until the soapy residue disappears.

I place the plate in our dish drying rack, otherwise known

as the broken dishwasher. Life would be so much easier if this thing worked! But no, my parents won't buy a new one. Maybe they can't afford it. Maybe they think they can fix it. Maybe doing dishes by hand reminds them of the good old days back in Eritrea.

The blind community has horror stories of blind kids who never contribute around the house because their parents tell them they can't. My parents expect me to do chores, and I do. Most chores have tactile elements that make them easy to do blind.

TT walks around me and stands on my left. Guessing she has something to say, I turn off the faucet and face her.

"What are you doing?" she asks.

"I'm doing the dishes."

"Dude, I'm not stupid. You never just offer to do the dishes. What are you really doing?"

I lower my voice. "Do you think they suspect anything?"

"No! They're too busy watching *Crocodile Hunter*. You know how Saba and Girma love that show."

"You like it, too. How come you stopped watching?"

"There's a commercial, and I wanted to find out what you're up to. So, what's up?"

"Okay...Don't tell them, though. I just joined this club called buildOn that builds schools in developing countries. They're going to do a trip to Mali to build a school, and I want to go. I need Girma or Saba to sign the permission form."

"Dude, they're gonna say no. You know they're gonna say no."

"But after I finish all these dishes, they'll have to thank me."

"Ha! More like if you do them for a whole year."

I smile. She gets it. Persuading our parents to let us step out-side their comfort zone is like climbing Kilimanjaro.

Following her lead, I join in the jesting. "Or they might let me go if I can find a cousin in Mali."

"Right?" TT giggles. "Just find one Eritrean in Mali. Then they'll say, 'Hey, we're related!'"

"Exactly. It always goes like that. That'll be my Plan B."

"So you're still gonna do the dishes?"

I consider it for a moment. My parents expect me to work hard at school and at home. The fact that I'm doing the dishes won't register as a big deal, but it may make them more recep-tive to my request. "Yeah, I'm still doing the dishes. Don't tell Saba and Girma my plan, okay? I want to tell them myself."

"Okay."

We fight about a lot of things, but TT and I are always on the same team when it comes to our parents. I know I can trust her.

The dishes beneath my hands shift around. TT has slipped two more plates in the sink.

"Hey!"

She runs out of the kitchen, chortling all the way.

Twenty minutes later, I place the last dish in the dishwasher. My arms and back ache. The soap and warm water shriveled my poor braille-reading fingers.

This time I walk right up to the big couch. One person is on the right and another is on the left. As I begin to sit down on the middle spot, I notice Saba's legs stretched out over the cushion. She moves her feet without me asking.

"Did you finish the dishes?" Saba asks.

"Yes! I did eight spoons, two knives, four bowls, six plates, and ten cups."

"Oh my god! Haben, you didn't have to count!"

I shrug. "I wanted you to know how hard I worked."

"Thank you, Haben," she says. "I appreciate that."

I beam at her. "You're welcome."

Girma chimes in from the other side. "Did you finish your homework?"

"Yes. Don't worry, I'm gonna get straight A's just like last year. Right now in world history we're learning about Japan."

"Okay. What's the capital of Japan?" he asks.

"Tokyo. I've known that for years." I search for a hard one. "What's the capital of Estonia?"

"That's easy. Tallinn. What's the capital of Chile?"

"Oh come on! Santiago. What's the capital of Indonesia?"

"Jakarta. And...what's the capital of Thailand?"

"Bangkok. What's the capital of Mali?"

"Bamako. And..."

"What do you think of Mali?" I can feel my heart speeding up as I try to act casual.

"Mali is an important country in Africa. Timbuktu is there, which used to be a huge trade center. Merchants from Africa and the Middle East would sell their goods in Timbuktu."

"That's so cool! What else do you know about Mali?" I prompt.

"They have great music. I love their music. I actually have a CD by a Malian singer."

I struggle to keep my expression contained, neutral, indif-

65

ferent. "How would you like it if I brought you a CD from Mali?"

"What do you mean?" He sounds suspicious.

I take a deep breath. "I joined a club called buildOn at school. It's part of a national nonprofit that builds schools in developing countries. They also do local community service. In April they will send a group of students to Mali for three weeks to build a school. It's completely free, they pay for the airfare, hotel, food, everything. All you have to do is sign the permission form."

Silence.

"Everything will be taken care of by buildOn," I reassure him. "I already filled out the application. You just need to sign the form—it's easy."

Silence.

"If I bring you the form, will you sign it?"

"Why do you want to go to Mali?" Girma responds, finally.

"I want to help build a better world. I want to help make sure kids in Mali get an education."

On my other side, Saba jumps in: "Haben, kids in Eritrea need schools, too. Why don't you help build a school in Eritrea?"

"Well…" I fumble around in my head looking for a response. "BuildOn doesn't go to Eritrea. If there were a program that builds schools in Eritrea, then I'd do that."

"Great idea," Girma says. "Next time we go to Eritrea, we'll find a school where you can volunteer."

"I'd be happy to volunteer at a school in Eritrea," I tell them. "We can plan to do that for our next summer vacation. But the buildOn trip is in April. I have time for both. I want to do both."

"Aren't you supposed to be in school in April?" Girma demands.

"BuildOn is a school club, and some of the teachers go with us, too."

Silence, again.

"How about this: if you let me go on this trip to Mali, I promise to volunteer at a school in Eritrea next summer."

"No way," Girma says.

"Why not?" My spirits drop. TT was right. They're not moved by my dishwashing.

"It's not safe," he answers.

"Mali is safe. BuildOn has been taking students there for several years. They only take students to safe countries."

"What about your disability?"

I brace myself for a tricky conversation. Guiding him through his disability fears requires summoning up enough courage for all of us. My own fears need to stay hidden. Any sign of nervousness on my part will trigger their protective instincts. The production of courage for three people, my parents and I, feels draining. I've been doing it more and more; my steps toward independence keep bringing up their fears for my safety. They raised me with stories of their long, arduous journeys to freedom, and I'm determined to reach for mine, too. "What about my disability?"

"How are you going to build a school when you can't see?"

"With shovels. With bricks. With hammers and nails. Just like everyone else. I don't know how to build a school, but the other American students don't know, either. We'll have teachers to show us what to do. I'll learn on the job just like everyone else, *with* everyone else."

"Haben, I've been to villages. I know what it's like. It's not safe," he says.

"You've been to villages in Africa and you survived just fine. If you can do it, I can do it."

"Haben," Saba calls for my attention. "There are kids in Eritrea who need schools. Why don't you help them?"

Flabbergasted, I just stare at her. Then, I search for the surest way to settle this once and for all. "Yes, I would be happy to volunteer in Eritrea *over the summer*. Right now, we're talking about me going to Mali in April."

I turn back to Girma. "The village is safe. The organizers have already checked it out. I promise, we'll be fine."

"Haben, I told you, it's dangerous. You could be walking on a path and not see a snake. Then what?"

My stomach clenches. He's right: I wouldn't see the snake. By the time I noticed, my body would be engulfed in pain.

"Oooh! She doesn't like snakes," says Saba triumphantly. "You got her good, Girma! See, Haben, you should just build a school in Eritrea."

"Saba!" My frustration boils over. "Eritrea has snakes, too!"

"No, the snakes there don't bite. If they see you they'll just think, 'Oh, she's Eritrean. I'll leave her alone.'"

I laugh and laugh, utterly floored by her fairylandish depiction of Eritrea. "Did you hear what she just said?"

"Yup," he chuckles. "Do you believe her?"

"It's true!" Saba insists. "They can tell when you're Eritrean.

Actually, we never see snakes in Eritrea. They tend to keep their distance from people."

I decide to play along. "Sounds like a great story for *Animal Planet*: Eritrea, the only country in the world where snakes never bite people."

Saba laughs. "Yeah, they should do a story. But they might bite you if you're not Eritrean."

"Uh huh." I nod and turn back to Girma. "There are snakes everywhere. In Eritrea. In Mali. In the Bay Area. I can't stop going into our backyard just because of the small risk that there may be a snake. I don't want to live a life of fear. I want to live a life of adventures. I want to go on this trip to Mali and help build a school."

"I don't think it's safe. Hey, TT! Do you know what your sister just said?"

She sits in an armchair. "What?"

"She's saying she wants to go to Mali."

"That's great!"

"Don't say that!" Girma protests. "It's not safe. She could get malaria. She could get kidnapped."

"Then you'll have to pay up the ransom."

"I don't have any money."

TT drawls, "It was nice knowin' ya, sista."

"TT!" Girma scolds. "How could you say that?"

"It's a joke!" She storms off to her room, and I feel guilty for getting her involved.

"Don't worry," I reassure Girma. "It will be safe. They've checked the village. They're working with the village leaders. I'll be with other students and teachers. I'll be fine."

"I don't like it. You're not going."

"But *why?*"

"I told you, it's not safe. You're not going. End of discussion."

My temples throb with a raging headache. My parents' fears wrap around me like a tight chain. They may never, ever let me grow up.

I stand up and walk away from the sofa, pausing at the edge of the living room to deliver my parting blow. "That's the last time I do the dishes."

My parents holler back, their voices serving as the soundtrack for my exit march.

I climb onto my bed, fuming at my stubborn parents. I explained everything so clearly: that we would be safe, that they wouldn't have to pay for the trip, but they still wouldn't budge.

I'm trapped, held back from doing my part to help others. The pain of their refusal squeezes my neck, threatening to spill over into tears.

Getting off the bed, I stand up and stretch my hands toward the ceiling. Bringing my hands down, I roll my head to the left. To the right. My neck begins to relax.

My life belongs to me. I can't surrender to feeling trapped.

Girma doesn't want to sign the forms because he thinks it's not safe for me to go. He brushed aside all of my arguments. My good, clearheaded, logical arguments. Maybe he thinks I'm biased and I'm exaggerating my abilities. But I *know* my abilities, better than anyone else. I'm the expert when it comes to what I can and can't do. My expertise didn't sway him, though.

The question then, is: who can convince Girma that I will be safe in Mali?

Two weeks later, I'm still hard at work on Operation Get My Parents to Say Yes. Every day, I have asked them to sign the form, approaching the issue from different angles each time. They're tired of the question. Girma has switched from saying, "No," to, "We'll see," a trick for bringing arguments to a halt. His strategy has had limited success. After all, I got my stubbornness from him.

Today, I'm using a different approach. I've invited my parents and the buildOn program manager for "just lunch." We're at Asmara Restaurant in Oakland, named after the capital city of Eritrea. I chose it as the site for my next move because my parents' favorite thing to eat is—surprise, surprise—Eritrean food. We take our seats—Girma on my left, and Saba across from him. Sitting across from me is Abby.

Abby has been leading buildOn treks for several years, taking high school students to places like Nicaragua, Haiti, and Nepal. Every week, she visits my high school's buildOn club where we plan our fundraisers, the trek to Mali, and local volunteer work. The other weekend, I volunteered to carve pumpkins at a retirement center. Before the session, I took Abby aside for a heart-to-heart. Explaining that my parents worried about my safety in Mali, I asked if Abby could meet them over lunch and convince them that I would be safe. She agreed. That day, the seniors got a pumpkin with a huge grin.

Inside Asmara Restaurant, Abby and my parents discuss Eritrean history. Abby seems fascinated, engaging my parents with thoughtful questions about their experiences. I keep busy eating, strategically staying quiet to maximize their bonding time.

"The way you eat, Abby! You're doing great," Saba says.

I beam at Abby. For the novice, Eritrean food requires a bit of training. The food is served on a large family-style plate covered with a spongy flat bread called *injera*. Depending on what people order, there might be meat stews, veggie curries, or salad on the main plate. We eat with one hand. Using the dominant hand, we tear off a piece of *injera*, about two inches in diameter, place it over a choice portion of meat or vegetable, and lift the *injera* and chosen food to our mouths.

"I've had Ethiopian food before," Abby explains.

"Eritrean and Ethiopian food are really the same," I tell her.

"No!" Saba's indignant. "They're not the same. They are similar, but not the same at all."

"That's right," Girma affirms. "They're similar. The dishes have different names. In Ethiopia, the names are in Amharic; in Eritrea, they are in Tigrinya. The style of eating is similar, and the way they cook it is similar."

I nod, smiling at his diplomacy.

"In Mali, we'll have lots of great food, too," Abby assures them. "We'll hire a cook to prepare meals for our team. Rice and vegetables. Beans. Chicken. Sometimes we'll get a goat. You won't have to worry about Haben eating well there."

"I see," Girma mumbles.

Silence.

I shoot anxious glances at my parents. Deep down, we know this isn't just about Mali. Mali is merely the first of many instances in which my parents will struggle to accept my independence. I don't want their fears to direct where I go in life, especially when I don't even allow my own fears to hold me back. If I survive Mali, my parents will start learning to trust me.

"But Abby..." Saba pauses before continuing. "How is she going to build a school?"

"She can do it. I don't know exactly how, but we'll find a way. I've seen her doing volunteer work in Oakland—she'll do just fine in Mali."

My heart swells with gratitude. What a beautiful, thoughtful, and honest response.

"Girma, what do you think?" Saba asks.

"Are you going to be with her the whole time?" he asks.

"I'll be with the group the whole time. There will be three other teachers, and we'll all be keeping an eye on the students. Someone will always be around."

Silence.

They're making faces again. Their use of inaccessible communication frustrates me. People should just say how they feel.

"Well..." Girma starts, "what about malaria?"

"We'll all be taking anti-malaria medication. They'll be fine."

I hold my breath. Please don't ask her about snakes. Please, please don't bring up snakes.

"Saba, what do you think?" Girma asks, handing the conversation back to her.

"Well, as long as Abby is with her, I think it's okay."

"Haben, are you sure you want to do this?" he asks.

"Yes, I'm very sure."

He sighs. "Okay, then. It's fine with me."

My heart dances salsa. He said *yes*! They both said yes! My persistence, my stubbornness, my careful planning—it all paid off.

"Great! We'll be happy to have Haben on our team," Abby says.

"Thank you, Abby," I gush. "Thank you for having lunch with us."

Chapter Eight

Water Fights in the Desert

Kegne Village, Mali. Spring 2004.

The Malian sun creates a scorching, brutal heat, even here in the shade. Abby and I rest in the shade of a tree as Ho Ying, another student, shovels desert sand through a sieve. The shovel makes a jarring swoosh as it slides into the sand.

"You're doing great!" Abby calls to her. Ho Ying is a sophomore, like me, and attends school in San Francisco.

It's our second day in Kegne Village, in southern Mali. Mali is a landlocked country in West Africa and includes a portion of the Sahara Desert. The Malian Empire was a thriving center for mathematics, the arts, and trans-Saharan trade, until France colonized Mali in 1892. Mali regained its independence in 1960. The official language is still French, but Bambara is the most widely used language. Like most of Mali, Kegne Village is a predominantly Muslim agricultural community.

Someone walks over to our tree. "Are you guys drinking your

water?" It's Simone. She's a sophomore at a high school in Berkeley.

Abby lifts her water bottle. "Haben, let's drink."

My eyebrows knit in confusion. I've already been drinking, but okay. Hefting my large water bottle, I slide the top open and begin to drink. We need to consume at least a liter of water every hour to stay hydrated. Perhaps Simone is making the rounds reminding everyone.

There are eleven of us American high school students. We traveled together from the Bay Area on this Trek for Knowledge. The program includes language lessons, cultural immersion, and of course, building a school.

"Haben, are you ready?" Abby stands up.

"You bet!" I follow her to the sand pile.

Ho Ying hands the shovel to Abby and returns to the shade.

"Here's the shovel." Abby presents me with the handle, and my right hand wraps around it. I nod, letting her know to continue. My dad taught me how to use a shovel years ago, so I feel prepared.

"Here's the sieve." She taps the shovel against the sieve, then slides the blade across the surface. "It's about three feet wide and four feet tall." The shovel and Abby begin moving to the left. Still holding the shovel handle, I take a few steps to the left. "Here's the pile." She plunges the shovel into a large pile of sand. "I want you to scoop up sand and drop it through the sieve."

"Okay." I nod again.

Holding the shaft with my left hand while my right hand grips the handle, I lift the shovel from the pile. Through my hands I feel the weight of the sand and rocks on the blade. Stepping to the right, I move the blade through the air until I feel it touch the sieve. Tilting the shovel to the right, I dump the blade's contents through the sieve.

"Great! Keep doing that." Abby walks back to the shady spot and sits down with Ho Ying.

I push the shovel into the pile again.

I can do this.

The blade taps the sieve, and I pour the contents through.

I'm building a school!

Sinking the blade into the sand pile, I lift, step, and toss the contents through the sieve. I launch my shovel back into the pile, beginning the process all over again. My mind and body settle into the routine. Beads of sweat drip down my face and back.

I'm competent. I'm capable. I'm building a school!

"Okay, that's enough. Let's switch," Abby says.

Slipping into the shade feels so refreshing. The heat here triggers exhaustion faster than the physical work. I guzzle water until I have to stop and breathe.

Over the course of the next hour, Abby, Ho Ying, and I take turns sifting sand.

"We're going to switch jobs now," Abby tells us. "We're going to go make bricks and another group will come here and sift more sand."

"So the sifted sand is used to make bricks?" I ask.

"Exactly."

"Cool. Can I get more water? My bottle is empty."

"Yeah, me, too," Ho Ying adds.

Abby leads us to the large tent. Dozens of people work under the tent, their bodies and movements all a blur. Abby stops at a small table and takes my water bottle from my hand. She unscrews the lid, pours some water, closes the top, and hands it back to me. She fills Ho Ying's bottle next, then her own.

"I'm going to go check with Fatima." Abby walks into the swarm of people under the tent. Fatima, a Malian, is buildOn's local partner with many hats: translator, cultural liaison, construction manager, and much more.

Several minutes later, Abby returns. "Ho Ying, come with me."

I continue standing by the table, wondering what to do next. Before me appears a maze of construction material and the foggy shapes of people working. Behind me stretches desert sand as far as I can see—which, admittedly, isn't very far.

The heat weighs down on my skin like several layers of wool sweaters. Raising my water bottle, I gulp down more water.

Abby suddenly pops up beside me. "Haben, you've been drinking a lot today. Do you have a drinking problem?"

I grin. "It's this heat. It makes me want to drink all the time."

"I'm gonna have to keep an eye on you, girl."

I laugh. "What can I do now?"

"Now we're making bricks. Follow me." Abby walks deeper into the tent. All around us people are shouting and laughing. "This is Oumar." Abby stops next to a tall guy. "You're going to work together to make bricks. I'll be going around checking on everyone. Are you okay?"

"Yeah."

"Awesome," Abby pats me on the shoulder. "Good luck!"

I look up at Oumar.

He talks, his words tumbling together.

I raise my hands in the universal sign of incomprehension.

He guides my hands to a pole. His hands are on the pole, too, just above mine. The pole moves, and vibrations travel up from the bottom. My hands listen. The pole bangs against a small container, a container with a thick liquid.

Oumar removes his hands. I continue stirring. The liquid sits in a two-foot-by-one-foot container. As I stir, I wonder what, exactly, are the contents of the container. Sand and water? Cement? Concrete?

Oumar calls to me. I face him and raise my eyebrows. He sets the pole aside, then he crouches down by the short side of the container. Understanding hits me. I move to the opposite side, bend down, and grasp the edges of the container. I feel the container lift. My hands flow with the movement of the container, responding to Oumar's shifts and turns. The container becomes an extension of his hands as we dance into the sun.

We deposit the container in a field of baking bricks, then walk back into the tent. Oumar pours different substances into a new container. He hands me the pole, and this time I know exactly what to do. I stir and stir and stir. I want him and all the Malians to know that I'm eager to help, even though I don't always know how. But stirring I can do. The thick liquid swirls in its container as I pull the pole around and around. Maybe they'll call me the Stirring American...

A voice shouts near my ear. "Haben!"

79

I jump. Still holding the pole, I nervously turn to face the speaker.

"I've told you twice already and you keep ignoring me! I'm just trying to help!" It's Simone again.

I take a deep breath. "Simone, I wasn't ignoring you. I didn't hear you."

"Then you should've asked me to repeat it. Why didn't you say you didn't hear me?"

"I literally couldn't hear you. I had no idea you were talking to me."

"Fine." She sounds unconvinced. "Are you going to drink now?"

My lips tense in a grim line. Handing off the pole to Oumar, I grab my water bottle, open the top, take a sip, and close it.

"That's not enough."

I stare at her with shock. Why is she picking on me? Fingers stiff with fury, I open the top, chug some water, and shut the lid. Putting the bottle down, I turn my back on Simone and resume stirring.

"Haben, I'm just trying to help you. Abby asked me to make sure everyone drinks lots of water. You could get dehydrated. Just don't wait until you're thirsty—if you're thirsty, you're already dehydrated."

My hands grip the pole. "Simone, I know how to drink water."

"I'm just doing my job," she says, already walking away.

The pole bangs around the container as I stir. I don't need reminders! Do they all think I'm incompetent?

Let go of the anger, I tell myself; the fear, the resentment. It's not worth the energy I should be spending on stirring.

My hands relax on the pole as I stir away my frustration. I need to remember to stay humble. I'm a fifteen-year-old raised in the Bay Area; of course there are things I don't know about staying hydrated in desert-like environments, and that's okay.

Sighted or blind, Deaf or hearing, each of us holds just the tiniest fraction of the world's wisdom. Admitting we don't know everything will aid us on this Trek for Knowledge.

Chapter Nine

Lost in the African Night

Kegne Village, Mali. Spring 2004.

"Want to play Go Fish with our host family?" I ask Ho Ying.

"Sure," she says. "But how are we going to teach them how to play? We can't speak Bambara."

It's our second evening in Kegne Village. Despite a long day of working in the field, I feel restless. Our eight-by-eight-square house has mud-brick walls on all four sides. We're sitting on the only piece of furniture in our room—a large wooden bed, with our sleeping bags underneath us to function as mattresses. We sleep on top of them since it's so hot here, even at night.

"I know the numbers in Bambara," I tell her.

"Okay, but can you teach them the game if you just speak numbers?"

"Maybe. We can try, right?"

"I guess . . ."

I scramble off our bed and kneel before my duffel bag on

the floor. Fear crawls up my arm as I unzip the bag. The zipper should keep the critters out, but I still feel apprehensive sticking my hand inside. My hand feels shirts, pants, soap...I pull out the small box of cards, then zip the bag shut.

"Hey, how's it going in here?" Abby and another person are standing in our open doorway three feet to my left.

"We're good." I stand up, holding the cards in my hands. "We're thinking about playing Go Fish with the kids. Do you think one of the translators could help?"

"Ibrahim is here with me and he can help for a bit, but after that we have to go check on the others. I see you already have cards. Lead the way."

Stepping outside into the warm evening, I turn to Ibrahim. "Can you ask the kids if they want to play a game?"

"Sure. Where will you play?" His accent is vaguely familiar, reminding me of my family in the eastern part of the continent. The accent is definitely easier than the British ones at camp.

"Here." I point to a lone chair in front of our house. "Can you ask if they can bring more chairs so we can all sit?"

Ibrahim walks over to another house ten feet away. Loud voices carry over to me. I know they must be speaking Bambara, but my ears can only classify speech into two categories: comprehensible or incomprehensible.

Kids and adults appear in front of our house, some running, some carrying chairs. I gesture to them to put the chairs in a circle. Ho Ying, four of the kids, and I sit in the six chairs. A circle of ten people stare down at us, chatting and laughing with the kids.

Ibrahim translates my explanation of the game as I pass out

cards. "Okay, they understand," he says. He and Abby then leave.

"Do you want to start?" I ask Ho Ying.

She looks down at her cards. "How do you say nine in Bambara?"

I silently count on my fingers. *Kele, fila, saba, nani, duru, wuru, woolanfla, shegin*... "*Kononton.*"

"*Kononton*," Ho Ying says to a kid across from her. "*Kononton?*" She points at the kid. "*Kononton?*" She holds up a card, points at the card, and then points at the kid. "*Kononton? Do you have kononton?*"

My face lights up in amusement. Sitting here reminds me of my days playing piano with the kids in Asmara. "Maybe they don't have that card?" I turn to the kid. "Say, 'Go Fish.'"

"Go feeesh!" a girl yells.

Ho Ying takes a new card from the main deck.

"Your turn. Ask anyone," I tell the girl. My hand gestures around the circle. I listen, waiting to see if the girl does anything. "Your turn." I point at her.

"*Wuru*," she says.

I give Ho Ying a quizzical look. "Who is she asking?"

"You."

I laugh. My left hand holds my cards as my right index finger skims the top left corner of each card, searching for a six. Several months ago, I inserted a regular deck of cards into a braille typewriter, embossing the number and suit on the top left corner of each card. My family and friends play lots of card games, so my hands have plenty of experience fanning cards out with my left hand while my right reads them, all while holding the cards vertically so that the other players can't see them.

"She's holding up a six," Ho Ying says. "Do you have a six?"

"Here is *wuru*." I hold my card out to the girl, and she takes it. "I'm going to ask for her name. *I togo?*"

The girl says something and they all laugh. I give Ho Ying another quizzical look. "What did she say?"

"I'm not sure." Ho Ying leans forward in her chair. "*I togo?*" Several kids shout responses. "I think they're saying... Kanja?" The group giggles.

"Kanja, your turn." Smiling, I gesture around to the whole group. "Ask someone. It's your turn."

Kanja and several people have an animated conversation.

"She's holding up a jack," Ho Ying says.

"Who is she asking?"

"You."

I fan out my cards in search of a jack. I pull it out and hand it to Kanja.

The kids continue to chatter around us. I hear Kanja say, "*Woolanfla*," meaning seven.

"She's asking you for a seven," Ho Ying announces.

My right index finger skims over my cards. "Here's *woolanfla*." I hand it over to Kanja. "You're doing great!" I smile and clap my hands.

"*Saba*," I hear from somewhere behind me. That's my mom's name. It's also the number three in Bambara.

"*Saba!*" Kanja shouts.

I spin around. Five people are standing behind me, reading over my shoulder. "Stop!"

They laugh. The kids in the circle laugh, too.

I stand up, waving my arms in a shooing motion. "No! *Ayi! Ayi!*" The little group parts, chortling as they step away.

Sitting down, I turn to Ho Ying. "They've been reading my cards out loud!" I check behind me. "Can you tell me if they come back? Next time I see Ibrahim I'm asking him how to say 'cheaters.'"

"Should we start over? Those points she just got don't really count."

"True…" I whirl around. Two people are standing behind me. "No! *Ayi!*" They back away.

These kids! They're not stopping! I can't keep looking over my shoulder.

"You know what?" I remember stirring away my frustrations after the tense exchange over the simple act of drinking water. "Maybe I failed to fully explain the game, or something got lost in translation. It doesn't matter who wins, really. The kids are having fun. I was having fun, too, until these guys—" I spin around and give them a warning look. They laugh. "We could make this part of the game. Go Fish and Spy."

"I guess… but I can't see their cards."

"Me neither." I giggle.

"*Saba!*" The kids start chanting. "*Saba! Saba! Saba!*"

"She's holding up a three," Ho Ying says.

I shake my head, more amused than anything. "Here." I pass her my three.

Ho Ying and I continue playing with the kids. Every few minutes I spin around and shoo away the spies. When I turn my back, they return to their positions at my shoulder.

Kanja—surprise, surprise—wins the game. We play three more rounds, and different kids win those. They work together, gathering and sharing information. The kids beat us at our own game.

"I'm tired," Ho Ying says. "Let's tell them we're done."

"*Ka su hɛɛrɛ!*" Goodnight, I tell the kids. Ho Ying and I start collecting the cards. When we have all of them, I wave farewell to the group before stepping into our house. "We'll play more tomorrow. *I ni ce.*" Thank you.

Soon after Ho Ying and I close our door, someone knocks. Ho Ying opens it, and I join her. Two adults stand in our doorway. "Come. *Dansi,*" one of them says.

"Do you recognize them?" I ask Ho Ying.

"One of them is our host father. I don't remember his name."

"Yosef."

"*Dansi,*" he repeats. "Come."

Ho Ying waves her hands and shakes her head. "No, thank you."

"Come. *Dansi.*" He points to our right, to a road that runs through the village.

Shaking my head, I take a step back. "*Ayi.*"

Yosef plays his walking stick like a guitar. "Come! *Dansi.*" He puts his walking stick down and dances around it.

My resolve melts. "What if he's trying to tell us that our friends are at a dance. I heard that they sometimes have dance parties here."

"But Abby would have told us if there was a dance party, wouldn't she?"

"Maybe they asked our host family to send us the message. It could be a spontaneous thing. I want to go—do you want to come?"

"Well...Okay."

"*Awo*," I tell him *yes*.

Ho Ying and I step outside, closing the door behind us. The second guy walks away. Yosef turns right, toward the road, leading us down a path we've never traveled before. We walk beside him, curious, intrigued, Ho Ying's flashlight illuminating the path ahead.

We walk on a dirt road that seems to stretch forever. Far on my left, I can see the tall outlines of trees. To the right, the open bush. A light breeze soothes my skin, making the temperature just right.

"*Bolo*." Yosef points to the sky.

"*Bolo?*" I look up. The dark sky sparkles with billions of stars. The specks of light look closer here than in the Bay Area. Somehow, my vision allows me to see stars, yet I can't even see Yosef's smile. Sight works in mysterious ways.

"*Wolo*," Yosef points at the sky again.

"*Wolo?*"

"*Lolo*." He points at the sky.

"*Lolo?*"

"*Awo*," he affirms.

"*Lolo*." I point at the stars, too. "Stars."

Yosef speaks, and I can't quite hear what he says.

"Stars," I repeat.

"Stars."

"*Awo!*" I laugh with delight.

We continue walking, Ho Ying on my right, and Yosef with his walking stick on my left. After a while, Yosef points to the sky again. "*Alo.*"

"*Alo?*" I ask.

"*Malo.*"

"*Malo?*" Exhaustion sweeps over me. The long day of working in the field, learning a new place, teaching the kids Go Fish, and now straining to hear Yosef—it piles up. Pushing myself through the constant stream of unknowns has drained all my energy.

"*Yalo,*" Yosef points again.

I shrug and shake my head.

We walk in silence down the road, trekking farther and farther from the village. The tall trees vanished long ago, back near the start of our journey. Ho Ying's flashlight illuminates a flat emptiness stretching all around us, and beyond that, a heavy darkness full of unknowns. Stories from my parents creep into my thoughts: lions, hyenas, and snakes.

"Where is he taking us?" Ho Ying asks.

My throat tightens, but I try to stay calm. "I don't know."

"There's no one out here!" Ho Ying sounds upset. "I haven't seen a house in a long time."

While preparing for this trip, I read stories about men who steal kids from villages, forcing them to work on plantations. My heartbeat rockets to a full panic. What if he's kidnapping us? He could be looking forward to a handsome payment from the plantation owners. He could have told us all this and we simply didn't understand, just as we don't understand where we're going.

"Maybe we should turn back," I suggest. "All we have to do is follow the path back."

Ho Ying stops and swings her flashlight back toward the way we came.

Yosef points his walking stick forward, gesturing for us to continue. My breath catches as I realize that he may have multiple uses for his "walking" stick.

Ho Ying turns, shining her light forward. "I think I see a compound up ahead."

The path brings us to a village studded with small, one-room houses just like ours. Their presence feels like protection from the open bush that stretches for miles all around us. I relax a bit. Here, at least, there are people within shouting distance.

Yosef steers us through the maze, weaving around houses. Up ahead, a huge light emits smoke and heat—a fire. As we come to a stop right in front of it, I notice a group of people sitting around the scorching flames. Several of them stand up and greet Yosef. They direct greetings to Ho Ying and me, but we shrink away. What now? Who are they? What are they going to do to us?

One man walks up to Ho Ying and me. He points to a house next to the fire. Yosef points at the house, too. Both men put their hands together, tilt their heads, and rest their heads on their hands.

Terror squeezes my heart. "They want us to sleep there!"

"I'm not sleeping in there! Whose place is that?"

"I don't know! I'm not sleeping there, either!"

Ho Ying is shaking her head and waving her hands. "No, no, no!"

I step back from the men. "No!" Yosef has crossed a line. There is no excuse for this. No cultural misunderstanding, no language barrier, no possible explanation for thinking two girls would agree to sleep in a random house. The Bambara word for no comes rushing back to me. *"Ayi! Ayi!"*

The door opens.

"Hey!" someone calls from inside. "It's Haben and Ho Ying! What are you guys doing here?"

"Zakiya!" Ho Ying rejoices. Zakiya is part of our group, another student from America. If this is her host family's house, then Jocelyn is probably in there, too. We're still in Kegne Village!

"Our host father brought us here," Ho Ying explains. "We didn't know you were here. What are you doing?"

"Jocelyn and I are trying to sleep. I just came out here because I heard a commotion."

"Sorry for waking you up," Ho Ying says. "Can you tell Yosef to take us home?"

"Sure!" Zakiya talks in another language. Maybe Bambara, maybe French.

Yosef leads us back, gliding through the maze of houses.

My feet drag on the ground as I trail behind him, every step pulsing with embarrassment.

The assumptions nondisabled people make about people with disabilities plague every aspect of my life. Turns out I need to check my assumptions, too. Anything can get lost in translation.

Chapter Ten

Guarding a Secret from the Village

Kegne Village, Mali. Spring 2004.

The construction site bustles with activity. Days of shoveling and brick-making in the intense heat have coated my skin in a layer of sweat and dust. The limited water supply here means we can only shower once a week.

"How's it going?"

A man's voice. I turn and then look up. His large sombrero adds to his height, tipping me off to his identity. Dennis is in his junior year at a Bay Area high school.

"Hey, Dennis. I'm, um..." My face goes hot with embarrassment. I don't want him to know what's going on. "Abby," I mumble. "I'm looking for Abby. Could you help me find her?"

"Yeah, I see her." Dennis disappears inside the construction tent.

I wanted to fix this problem myself, but now I'm committed to talking to Abby. Part of coming to Mali was to prove to my parents that I can take care of myself. Does asking for help count as taking care of myself? I'm still a competent, capable, responsible woman. Right?

Dennis arrives. "Here's Abby."

"Thank you." Guilt churns my stomach as I slowly turn away from him to face Abby. "Can I talk to you? Privately?"

"Privately, huh?" Abby leans in. "You have a secret?"

My face explodes with burning mortification.

"I'm just teasing! Okay, let me see where we can go." She leads the way out of the tent. We pass rows of bricks baking in the sun. About a hundred feet from the bricks, Abby stops by a tree. "All right, no one can hear us here."

"Okay. So..." I swallow.

"Let me guess—your water broke?"

"My water bottle works fine." I give her a puzzled look.

"Sorry, bad joke." She switches to a more serious tone. "What's going on, Haben?"

I take a deep breath. "Remember how you said everything we bring needs to be biodegradable? Soap, toilet paper, everything. Well, I did that." I breathe, summoning my courage to say it. "The biodegradable tampons I brought are not working."

"They're not working?"

"No." My face begs her to stop asking questions.

"Well, you know what the women here do, don't you?"

I blush. Abby stands there, waiting. "They use strips of cloth that they wash and reuse. If I have to, I could do that, but I really hope I don't have to. Can you help me?"

"I'll see what I can do."

"Thank you! I'll be okay either way. I'm capable of taking

care of myself. It's just that, if there's anything you could do, if you happen to have any extra products, I'd really appreciate it."

"Oh, I'm not worried about you. You're doing great. Now some of those other kids..."

I perk up. "What? Who? What did they do?"

She laughs. "Oh, Haben."

"Yes?"

"I won't say. But believe me, this is nothing. I'll see if I can find you anything. Can you keep working here?"

"I'd like a shower, if that's possible."

"Sure. I'll ask Fatima."

Abby goes to find Fatima, and the two women talk among themselves. I wonder how much Abby tells her. Asking for help feels like losing control of a situation. It increases the likelihood of a secret becoming public knowledge. I trust Abby and Fatima, though. The three of us will keep the information contained, and no one else will know.

Fatima and I walk back to the compound. A few trees line the road from the construction site to the village center. The trees remind me that, despite the horrendous heat, this isn't even the desert.

At the compound, Fatima talks with another woman. The woman leaves, then returns with a bucket.

"Okay, here is water," says Fatima. "You can use this for your shower."

"Is there a cup or something I could use to pour water from the bucket?" I ask.

"Yeah, it's in there."

"Okay, great." I smile. "So where do people shower?"

"You shower in the bathroom."

The bathroom is a small roof-less room comprised of four short walls and a hole in the ground. The open hole emits an awful stink that assaults any nose within ten feet. Inside the bathroom, the stench becomes a breath-stopping beast.

I try to hide my dismay. "Okay, I think I can take it from here. Thanks, Fatima." I turn to the other woman and thank her in Bambara. "*I ni ce.*"

I walk to my room, strolling by two other houses before I reach mine. It's a short walk—about thirty feet—one that I've completed many times. Drinking lots of water has its consequences.

I change from sneakers to flip-flops. Feeling through my duffel bag, I pull out clean clothes, a towel, soap, and a new frustrating, flimsy, biodegradable tampon. It was probably designed by men. Honestly, no woman would have designed something so important to be this useless.

Hugging my gear to my chest, I walk back to the bathroom. Stepping inside, the stench hits me like a physical force. I stop breathing. My lungs begin to hurt. I take a tiny breath, struggling to just breathe through my mouth.

It takes effort to accept the smell. I tell myself it's human.

I put my clothes and supplies on top of one of the brick walls. People have to squat over the hole to use it. Since the space is designed for squatting, the walls are only about five feet tall all around. I realize that people must have to squat while showering, too. Talk about awkward.

I step outside, take a huge gulp of air, and then haul the bucket into the stink room.

Later, Abby drops by my house. "How was your shower?"

"Hmm...the water felt refreshing."

"Awesome. I found you some rags."

My mouth starts to turn down in disapointment, then I catch that judgmental thought, reminding myself to respect the local customs.

"Thanks." Taking the bag, I turn it over in my hands. It's tampons! I laugh with relief.

"These should work better. If they don't, let me know and we'll figure something else out."

"Thank you!"

"You bet. Was that all? Do you need anything else?"

"Yeah, it would be nice to wash my clothes," I tell her. "I brought laundry soap. I just need more buckets of water."

"I can ask. I'm guessing you've washed clothes by hand before?"

"Yeah, in Eritrea. My grandmother had a washing machine, but she never used it. I think it was broken, or maybe it only worked when there was enough water in the water tank on the roof. I don't remember the exact reason, I just remember that we did all the laundry by hand."

"So you're a pro! Maybe you can do my laundry, too."

My face warms. "I'm not an expert or anything, but if you need tips, I could give you some."

Abby laughs. "I'm kidding! Let me go find you some buckets. I'll be right back."

Ten minutes later, I follow Abby to a bench stationed against the wall of the house next door. A woman is sitting there.

"She's offered to do your laundry for you," Abby explains.

If she does it, she'll know I'm on my period. And if she knows, the whole village will know!

"No, *ayi*." I shake my head emphatically. I point to myself and point to my bag of laundry.

The woman stands. She and Abby talk for a while, and then the woman leaves.

I breathe a huge sigh of relief. One of the articles I read said that some villages segregate women on their periods, sending them away to a separate part of the village. They wouldn't send me away, would they?

"Need anything else?" Abby asks.

"Nope, I'm good."

"Okay, see you later."

Pulling out a pair of pants from my bag, I dunk them into the first bucket and get to work.

Water splashes my arms as I wash, scrub, rinse, and wring. Cool, soothing, refreshing water. A scandalous thought pops into my head: I'm doing laundry *and* enjoying it!

Doing laundry blind is easy—it's all about having a system. Ideally, I would have a third bucket for a second rinse, but I don't want to use any more of my host family's water than is absolutely necessary.

I finish washing my clothes and lay them out on my bed to dry. The heat will dry them in an hour, maybe less. I carry the buckets behind the house and dump the dirty water. I feel happy knowing that the laundry soap is biodegradable.

A person walks by. A man, probably part of the host family. I hand him the buckets.

He takes the buckets and walks away. Five seconds later he marches over to me, yelling.

My heart jumps. Shame glues my feet to the ground as I contemplate the source of his fury.

He yells again, gesticulating with a bucket.

My arms rise and fall in a part question, part apology. "Sorry?" I remind myself that loud voices sound angry to me. This could all be a big misunderstanding.

Still shouting, the guy thrusts the bucket in my face.

Tilting my head, I peer down at the bucket. My eyes don't see anything amiss, so my mind searches for answers. Maybe he's mad I dumped the water? Maybe the laundry soap changed the color of the bucket? Maybe there's a red stain?

My body tenses with mortification, and my heart pounds wildly. He knows! The whole village will know!

This desperation to keep my period a secret has seeped into every interaction, triggering harmful and exhausting worries. I don't actually know why he's upset or what's wrong with the bucket. Some cultures stigmatize menstruation, but I can choose to embrace it. After all, almost every woman experiences menstruation.

I straighten my back, look up at the man, and use a strong, firm voice. "It's biodegradable."

Chapter Eleven

The Latrine

Kegne Village, Mali. Spring 2004.

"Hi!" I call over to the group. Two people rest in the shade of a tree while a third person sifts sand.

"Hey, Haben," the person closest to me says. "It's Simone and Elizabeth." Elizabeth is an English teacher at a high school in Berkeley. She's super thoughtful and is always ready to answer whatever questions I have.

I sit down on the sand next to them, grateful for the shade. "Guess what?"

"What?" Simone asks.

"I'm now your water boss. *So*, are you two drinking your water?" My playful tone masks the seriousness with which I take my job. I intend for the day to end with everyone still hydrated and still speaking to me. The memory of my impatience with Simone on our first day makes me cringe.

Simone and Elizabeth drink.

"I can't believe we're leaving tomorrow," Elizabeth says. "It's going to be so hard to leave. I'll miss working here with you guys. I'll miss my host family and playing with the kids."

"Me, too." I rotate the water bottle in my hands. "Do you think we can hang out in the Bay Area? When we get back?"

"Yeah, definitely!" Simone says. "You're really nice."

I give her a puzzled look. "You sound surprised."

"I didn't mean it like that! I guess I was kind of intimidated. I thought you were too smart and wouldn't want to be my friend."

"Simone, I don't think I'm smarter than you at all! Why would you think that? Did I do or say something?"

"I don't know, really. I think it's because back at the pre-trek meeting, whenever Abby asked a question, you always knew the answer."

I'm perplexed. "That's because I did the reading. All of her questions came out of the reading packet they gave us."

"That's the thing—no one else did the reading."

My eyes widen with disbelief. "Really?"

"Haben, you were the only one who knew the answers. No one else did the reading. There were so many articles. I meant to read it, I tried to read it, but I didn't have time..."

"I had no idea. Wow."

I try to process the news. The bulging packet had all kinds of articles in it, explaining the history of Mali, the basics of Bambara, the recommendations for eco-friendly travel gear...Wait a minute! If no one else read the packet, then was I the only one who brought biodegradable products? All this time, the other girls used their regular products while I suffered and struggled and sacrificed. This is the last time I ever read anything.

Simone continues, "You obviously did the reading, and I felt bad that I didn't, and I guess I just assumed you wouldn't like me because of it."

I sigh. "I can't see and hear as well as you do, so I had more to lose if I skipped the reading. I studied the materials because I wanted to be useful to the team—like a human version of Google."

"I didn't think about it that way."

The swoosh of the metal shovel sliding through sand fills the awkward silence.

I slowly stand up. "I should get back to work. Hey—I noticed a bunch of people going over there." I point to the left corner of the construction site. "What are they doing?"

"I don't know," Simone replies. "Want me to go with you?"

"Sure."

Simone turns to Elizabeth. "Is it okay if I go with Haben?"

"Yeah, that's fine. John and I will take turns sifting sand."

As Simone and I walk to the far-left corner of the work site, my eyes catch sight of a two-foot high brick wall. I'm swept away with awe—my hands made some of those bricks! My hours of shoveling, sifting, stirring, and sweating, created some of those bricks. In two months, this village will have a schoolhouse to serve eight hundred eager young learners, and the thousands to come after them. This fifteen-year-old Deaf-blind girl from Oakland has actually made a positive impact in the world. The realization gives me a boost of optimism.

We walk past the foundations of the schoolhouse and reach a group of people standing around. Simone chats with several of them while I look around, hunting for a visual or audio clue.

Fatima steps in front of me. "Haben, how about you?"

"Sorry?"

Fatima turns and faces the whole group. "Haben, no. Meisha, no. Simone, no. Only Dennis! Why aren't any girls helping?"

I call after her, "'Haben, no,' what?"

Someone else comes to my side. "Hey, it's Abby."

"Abby!" I pretend to scold her. "Are you drinking your water?"

She laughs. "Yes, ma'am."

"Great. What's Fatima talking about?"

"We're digging a hole to build a latrine for the school. Fatima is trying to get more people to help. So far it's just been men from the village and Dennis."

"I can help!"

"You want to help dig the latrine?"

I grin. "Yes!"

"Fatima!" Abby waves, and Fatima walks over. "Haben says she wants to help."

"Good! I'll let them know." Fatima walks away, calling out in Bambara as she goes.

I turn to Abby. "What exactly are they doing?"

"You mean you offered to help without knowing exactly what's involved?"

I laugh. "You know me. I always want to try everything."

"I love it. So, Dennis is down there right now. He has a pickax and he's breaking ground. Every so often they're shoveling out all the dirt."

Abby guides me to the edge of a rectangular hole that's about ten feet long and five feet wide.

"How deep is it?"

"It's about six feet down. Dennis, can you help her down?"

I don't need a guy to help me jump. My legs work just fine. I sit down at the edge, my legs dangling in the air. Peering in, I spot Dennis digging on the other side. Perfect, the coast is clear. I push off the ledge, launching myself into the pit.

Dennis catches me. Tilting me in his arms, he lowers me to my feet. The discovery that there are people with this kind of strength, speed, and coordination boggles my mind. It almost makes up for interrupting my jump.

My knees feel weak as I take a shaky step away from him. "Are you drinking your water?"

"I'll drink while you work," he says.

"Okay. Show me what to do."

Dennis bounces over to the other side of the hole, lifts the pickax, and hands it to me. The shaft of the pick has a coating of grime that now covers my palms. I continue exploring, following the long shaft to its head. After rotating the pick so that the sharp, pointy end faces down, I reposition my hands around its center.

Dennis steps behind me, reaches over, and places his hands on the pick next to mine. He slowly raises the pick over my right shoulder, then stretches forward as he brings the pick down on the ground in front of us. My salsa skills prove useful as I lift, step, and stretch along with the pick and Dennis. He lifts and pounds the ground again. And again.

The bubbly feeling under my skin continues spreading, tampering with my ability to breathe. I clear my throat. "Okay, I got it."

Dennis steps away, leaving the pick to me.

*   *   *

I raise the pick over my shoulder and bring it down in front of me. The swing feels easier now that I have the pick to myself. I lift it and smash it down again. Up, down. Up, down. The brutal sun beats down on us. Six feet beneath the surface of the earth, with no breeze, the pit becomes an oven. Beads of sweat slide down my face as I work. Up, down. Up, down. The ground crumbles with every blow, the pick digging deeper and deeper into the hard earth.

I shoot a quick glance over at Dennis. The tall figure with the large hat stands three feet away. I wish I could see his facial expressions. Is he watching me, or gazing at the crowd above the pit? Does he appreciate the chance to rest while someone else toils away? Does he mind sharing the work with a girl? Or maybe he sees me as just a disabled person.

I smash the pick against the defiant earth. The pick swings with the force of my whole body. My arms, my shoulders, my knees, my core, all work together as I lift and slam it down. My muscles ache with fatigue, but I push myself to keep breaking ground.

My arms reach their limit, and I pass the pick back to Dennis. He takes it and moves to the other side.

I scan the wall for a ladder. "How do I get out?"

An arm wraps around my back and another beneath my knees. My cheeks burn as Dennis raises me into the air, higher and higher, until I'm over his head. Reaching my hands out to the ledge, I roll onto solid ground.

Laughter ripples through the crowd as Abby kneels beside me. "Are you okay?"

"Yeah." I crawl away from the edge and stand up. "I wanted to get out by myself."

"It's pretty deep. Everyone's been getting a lift out."

"Oh." The news surprises me.

"You were great down there," Abby says. "You guys make a good team."

My pulse quickens. "We all make a great team."

"Hey, what's that look?"

I try to change my expression, then give up with a laugh. "You tell me your secrets and I'll tell you mine."

"Deal."

Chapter Twelve

Untangling Love and Control

Oakland, California. Summer 2005.

One August afternoon before the start of my senior year of high school, my parents corner me in my room. My mother, Saba, positions herself on the bed next to me while Girma, my father, takes the chair between me and the door.

"Haben, you should stay in the Bay Area for college." Saba holds my hand. "We know you're smart, but you can't go to college in another state."

"I'll be fine—I went to Mali."

"Listen to Saba," Girma pleads. "We don't have any family in Minnesota, or Massachusetts, or any of those other places. They're too far away."

I give him my best don't-worry-about-it smile. "I went to Mali."

"Stop saying that!" Saba jiggles my hand as if trying to shake some sense into me. "This has nothing to do with Mali. Okay? We're talking about college. You're a straight-A student; you could go to Berkeley. Or Stanford. Why don't you apply to Stanford? We'll bring you food every weekend. Home-cooked Eritrean food."

"Actually, I was just reading about an amazing school in New Zealand."

"Haben! *Oof.*" Girma stands up. "You're not listening!" He lets out a deep sigh of exasperation. "We'll talk to you later." With that, my parents walk out of the room, taking their fear with them.

I breathe a sigh of relief. If I stay here, all my energy will go toward managing their never-ending worries. I can't go dancing because they are too tired to drive me after a long day at work, and they don't want me taking public transit by myself because, "It's not safe." Their plan to chauffeur me conflicts with the exhaustion of their jobs—Girma is a lab technician and Saba is a nurse aide. An orientation and mobility teacher explained to them that I have the skills to take buses and subways on my own. They shook their heads and continued chanting, "It's not safe." Pursuing salsa lessons remains just a dream, alongside all the other dreams thwarted by my parents' fears.

They're right about one thing: college won't be like Mali. I won't have Abby brainstorming solutions with me. The way they see it, I won't have *anyone* with me. They personally experienced the pain of living in a new place without a community, and they don't want me to suffer through that.

How would I manage in college? How would I make it work?

Then, I realize the perfect solution: a guide dog! I'll get a guide dog the summer before I start college. Brilliant!

My computer pings with a message. It's from my friend Bruce, a college student and a leader in the National Federation of the Blind. I tell him about my plans to get a guide dog.

Bruce: You want to depend on a dog for confidence?

Haben: It sounds funny when you put it that way.

Bruce: Guide dog schools actually require applicants to have strong cane travel skills before they can get a dog. If a blind person doesn't have confidence, then the dog and person both end up lost. Don't depend on a dog for confidence. Build up your own confidence. Develop your skills at a National Federation of the Blind training center. I went to the one in Louisiana.

Haben: Why did you go to the one in Louisiana?

Bruce: It's the toughest. It's like blindness boot camp. The staff there have really high expectations. Many organizations that claim to help blind people have low expectations. One test to determine whether a center sets high expectations is to ask if the instructors themselves can do the lessons without sight. There are a lot of teachers for the blind who don't have blindness skills. I've heard of braille teachers who only read braille with their eyes. They can't read braille with their fingers.

Haben: Wow.

Bruce: It's frustrating for the students. There are also sighted cane travel instructors who could never navigate Times Square with their eyes closed, so they tell blind travelers it's not safe.

Haben: I bet I could walk through Times Square.

Bruce: You could apply to NYU and Columbia.

Haben: Well...Maybe.

Bruce: Scared?

Haben: No way! I went to Mali.

Bruce: I know. Whatever you decide, just remember that a guide dog won't teach you blindness skills.

Haben: Point taken.

Bruce: A blindness training center will help you develop more blindness skills. Depend on yourself for confidence. Confidence comes from within.

Haben: I love that! Confidence comes from within. Not from a dog. Not from a cane. Not from a boat. Not from a plane. Confidence comes from within.

After researching training centers, I decide to attend the Louisiana Center for the Blind. Spending one summer at an intensive blindness program will give me a whole lifetime of not having to wonder how blind people complete various tasks.

My parents won't like this plan. Increasing my independence skills will decrease their control over me. The thought of losing their ability to keep me in their comfort zone scares them. To their credit, they do give me more freedom than most parents of kids with disabilities. Many parents would never permit a disabled daughter to travel to Mali. I'm blessed to have parents who love me and work hard to provide a home for us. My gratitude exists alongside the persistent pounding of my heart to go, go, go.

Go, because dancing fills me with joy unlike sitting safely on the sidelines. Go, even though it means nights of crying myself to sleep. Go, because the stories of my family compel me to reach for the grand unknown, in all its hope-filled glory.

My parents will understand in the end. We can disentangle control from love. I'll convince them to let me attend this training center in Louisiana. At least I'm not going to New Zealand. Not yet, anyway.

Chapter Thirteen

The Chapter My Parents Shouldn't Read

Ruston, Louisiana. Summer 2006.

The Louisiana Center for the Blind (LCB) is located in this small town called Ruston. I flew here right after my high school graduation. LCB has about fifteen adults from all over the country with a variety of different life experiences. We all aim to sharpen our blindness skills. Students with some usable vision, like me, wear sleepshades—eye masks that block out light. Wearing sleepshades during class encourages us to learn nonvisual techniques rather than relying on our residual vision. Students need to know that they can meet their goals even in situations with poor lighting, or when that residual vision fades away.

The woodshop class has become my favorite. Every time I take command of the power tools, I feel like I'm redefining what it means to be a blind woman. The tools terrify some students. Not me. Hello, radial arm saw!

A firm flick of the switch and the roaring beast comes to

life. The thunderous spinning of the blade blocks out all other noise. The table trembles from the force, a force with the power to chop off a finger. Or more.

One hand holds a block of wood in place while the other grips the handle of the saw. I pull the saw handle, dragging the spinning blade through the block. My hand monitors the changing intensity of the vibrations coursing through the wood. Dust shoots up in all directions, engulfing my nose in the woodsy notes of independence.

Suddenly, the vibrations in the wood drop. It's cut!

Turning off the saw, I set the machine back into place. The block is four inches long, two inches wide, and two inches deep. Once I've drilled six holes and cut six pegs, the pegs on the block will form braille letters.

The woodshop instructor, JD, wants us to believe, really and truly internalize, that blind people can tackle "dangerous" tasks. We can develop safe, nonvisual techniques for just about anything.

My father loves tools, and as protective as he is, he actually taught me how to use hammers and screwdrivers. Not the electric saws, though. "It's not safe," he said, and I agreed.

JD wore sleepshades when he introduced me to the radial arm saw—he didn't need sight to teach me to use it. After a few exciting lessons, we both agreed that I could handle the saw on my own.

Holding my block in one hand and using my cane with my right, I walk back to the main worktable. The cane, about five feet long, extends from my hand to the ground in front of me. Gently tapping the cane left to right as I walk alerts me to objects. The cane soon taps against something solid, and from experience I know it's the table. I walk around the table until I feel my seat.

I hear the voices of JD and two students at the table, their words incoherent murmurs. Keisha, one of the students, shares an apartment with me. She grew up in Louisiana and just finished high school. The other student, Luke, is from Ohio. He's also a recent high school graduate.

I start using a tubular measuring device called a click rule. It emits a click every one sixteenth of an inch as its metal rod slides out of the tube. The rod has a knob at the top to lock it in place for a specific measurement. I count the tactile marks on the rod to calculate the exact placement of the six holes I need to drill on the block. The handy scratch awl, a pencil-like device for marking wood, leaves an indentation at each spot. Once I have all six spots marked, I proceed to the drill press.

If I were staying for the whole program, I could advance to making jewelry boxes, cabinets, grandfather clocks—anything really. Most students stay at the center for six to nine months, giving them plenty of time to complete large projects. Keisha and Luke are doing the full program, postponing the start of college. But I'm only here for the summer, so no jewelry boxes for me.

In cooking class, I make a meat loaf, then offer it to the other students. The cooking instructor promises to find a vegetarian recipe for our next lesson.

Only about ten percent of blind people can read braille. Text-to-speech software helps blind people access information, but it's not literacy. Some blind kids who only listen to books grow up thinking "once upon a time" is one word. Learning braille leads to reading and writing skills that boost future employment opportunities, so braille is a critical part of independence training at LCB. The instructor appreciates my braille reading skills. Every now and then he calls on me to read out loud to the other students, making the point that the blind can read to the blind.

In computer class, we master using the internet with a screenreader, a software application that converts graphical information on the screen to speech and digital braille. We operate the computer through keyboard commands instead of a mouse.

For the last class of the day, my travel instructor and I set off through the town of Ruston, navigating different kinds of street and railroad crossings. Trains rush through Ruston along a track right next to LCB. We're all used to it. The center helps students develop the skills to travel in all kinds of environments.

The long day of classes finally comes to an end. Outside, the humid, swampy, Southern heat hits me like a tall ocean wave.

"Hey! Who's this?" someone calls as their cane taps my shoes.

I turn around. "It's Haben."

"Haben! That meat loaf you made was so good."

"Thanks, Luke."

"You heading to the apartments, too?" LCB's student apartments are about a twenty-minute walk from the center's main building.

"Yeah." I swing my cane out and begin walking.

Luke walks beside me. He taps his cane to the left just as mine taps to the right. Crash! "Sorry!" Luke pulls his cane away. Stepping to his right, he creates more space between us.

"It's fine. It happens." I continue walking.

We stop at an intersection. Blind people cross streets safely by understanding traffic patterns. LCB's travel instructors take students to unfamiliar intersections and ask them to analyze the traffic sounds until they can identify the type of intersection: a light-controlled T intersection, a four-way stop sign, or could it be a busy parking lot? Parallel moving traffic sounds different from perpendicular traffic. Cars surging forward when the light turns green have a distinct sound, too.

Blind people with additional disabilities, like me, use other techniques. I often can't identify the direction of sounds, and I miss many sounds. My limited sight only allows me to see cars from a distance of ten feet or so—just enough to study the intersection from the safety of the sidewalk. I use a combination of these visual and audio clues. When those fail, I ask another pedestrian for assistance or walk to another intersection.

The intersection at the corner of LCB is a stop-sign-controlled T intersection. Our near parallel traffic rolls by, and I begin crossing the street, cane first. Luke walks beside me on my right. I maintain some distance to prevent our canes from crashing.

Luke says something. On the other side of the intersection, I ask him to repeat the question.

"What are you doing this evening?"

Loud railroad crossing bells begin ringing.

"Oh." I stop. Luke stops, too.

"Did you hear what I said?" he asks.

"Yeah." *What are you doing this evening.* What a loaded question! If I tell him "not much," he might think I'm boring.

"Well?"

I laugh, embarrassed. "I was just thinking I'd eat dinner and then read a book." Is he going to suggest something? God, this is awkward. "You know, we're like a block away from the tracks. Want to keep walking for a while?"

"Okay."

We start walking, canes tapping in front of us.

Luke speaks again.

"What?" I step closer. My cane collides with his. Pulling my cane away, I move to the left. There, about four feet between us. We should be able to walk and talk without hitting our canes.

Loud noise blocks out Luke's voice again. Frustrated, I abandon proper cane technique. Holding my cane off to the left, I scoot over to Luke. Walking shoulder-to-shoulder, I tell him, "Sorry, I didn't hear that."

"I asked"—Luke raises his voice—"where are you going to college?"

"Lewis & Clark College. It's a small liberal arts school in Portland, Oregon."

My cane covers just half the area in front of me, unable to sweep a full 180 degrees. Left, middle. Left, middle. I don't want to trip over a street pole. Or Luke's cane. Or an unpleasant surprise.

Luke responds.

"What?"

Left, middle. Left, middle.

I lean in, straining to hear as we walk.

"I said," Luke repeats himself, but I miss it again.

My cane scans for obstacles. Left, middle. Left, middle.

Looking left, I spot something huge heading toward us.

"Stop!" I reach for Luke's arm.

Luke steps forward, then rocks back. "What?"

The train blasts us with a powerful wind that shocks my skin. The ground shakes as the train roars by about two feet in front of us, creating an earthquake under our feet. The thunderous noise hurts my ears. Next to the towering machine, I feel fragile. Mortal.

Gripping Luke's arm, I pull us several steps back. My heart slams against my rib cage as I watch enormous car after enormous car zoom across the tracks in front of us.

Luke stomps his cane and hurls profanities at the retreating train. "We almost got killed!"

"I know," I whisper. My fingers are locked around my cane. I pry them loose, shaking out my hand.

"You saved my life."

My jaw drops. "I did not!"

"Yes, you did."

"No, I didn't." I feel like an irresponsible child, not a hero. "You might have noticed the sound of the train, or the ground shaking, or your cane might have reminded you about the tracks."

"It would have been too late."

My breath catches in my throat, and the ground under my feet seems to tilt. Trying to steady my nerves, I revert to joking.

117

"All right, you win. I saved your life." I manage a weak smile. "You owe me—big. What's it gonna be?"

"Well, uhhh...I can make really good spaghetti."

I laugh with surprise. "You're saying your life is worth a plate of spaghetti?"

"And garlic bread."

Smiling, I shake my head. "Can you cook for Keisha, too?"

"Of course."

"Great!" We'll have a delicious dinner. Dinner at the apartments. Apartments on the other side of those tracks...I take a deep breath. The bells are silent. Our parallel traffic is moving. "Ready to go?"

He raises his cane and swings it out in front of him. "Okay, yeah, let's go."

Tapping my cane ahead of me, I begin walking. My heart hammers when the tip of my cane touches the metal rails. I feel an urge to turn back, but I force myself to keep going. Then the rails press against the soles of my shoes, daring me not to fall.

When we reach the sidewalk on the other side, I stop. "Hey, Luke?"

"Yeah?" He stops walking.

"We almost got killed because we were distracted." I take a steadying breath, trying to keep my voice calm. "We knew a train was coming. There were so many signs—the bell, the sound of the train, the parallel traffic stopping, the vibrations through the ground. Blindness wasn't the problem. Sighted people get distracted, too. Many sighted people have been killed by trains. It's about paying attention, not blindness. Does that make sense?"

"Yeah."

"I hope it was okay for me to say that. I don't mean to lecture."

"It's fine."

"Okay. And thanks for offering to make dinner. That's really nice of you."

"It's a special recipe my dad taught me. It's really good."

Luke, Keisha, and I thoroughly enjoy the dinner Luke prepares for us. I don't mention the train, and neither does he.

Later, alone in my room, memories from the terrifying scene play through my mind. If my parents hear about this incident, they'll probably blame my disability. They might try to ban me from crossing tracks. Or crossing streets. Or going outside without them, period. Every time my mind wanders back to the tracks, a fiery bolt of guilt flashes through me. It feels like my single moment of distractedness has set back blind-kind by several decades. Many people will blame blindness, but those with disability literacy will recognize that carelessness created the danger.

Chapter Fourteen

Play Like No One's Watching

Ruston, Louisiana. Summer 2006.

I'm eating dinner with three older LCB students, hoping to absorb some of their wisdom. Tom is a fifty-year-old who works at a transportation company in Pennsylvania. He cooked dinner and invited a few students to his apartment. Mason, from Alabama, is learning blindness skills so he can enjoy retirement with dignity—he's in his seventies. The fourth person with us is Rosa, a woman in her forties who works as a teacher in Arizona. My age, seventeen, makes me the youngest person at the table.

"You, yeez people!" Rosa yells at Tom.

My eyebrows furrow in confusion. Admitting I don't know what she means would draw attention to my status at the table: the least experienced one, the naïve one, the kid. Accepting the risk, I voice my question, *"Yeez people?"*

"Y-E-A-S-T. Yeast," Tom clarifies. He's the easiest to hear

of the three. Mason is the hardest to hear. I don't think I've ever caught a single word from him.

"Oh, *yeast* people..." My voice expresses my bewilderment. "What does it mean?"

"She's been calling me that ever since the cooking class," Tom says. "Rosa asked how yeast makes bread rise, and I told her that it's because of the Yeast People."

"Tom!" I burst into incredulous laughter.

"That's why I call him Yeast People! He is the Yeast People!" Rosa says. Tom is the opposite of yeast-sized. He's around six and a half feet tall, walking with the longest cane at LCB.

I lean over to Rosa. "He lied about the Yeast People."

Tom pounds the table. "Haben, don't say that! There are Yeast People."

Rosa pushes her chair back. "Are you lying to me?"

Tom mumbles a response.

"You liar! I'm going to teach you a lesson." She stands up and starts walking around the table, making her way to Tom.

The table starts shaking as a large person crawls underneath. Tom!

The room dissolves into hysterics. Mason clambers out of his chair and starts hollering with Rosa. I stay in my seat, laughing so hard my sides hurt. A blind man dove under a table to hide from a blind woman!

Rosa and Mason have a heated conversation. Then Rosa yells, "Haben!"

"Yes, Rosa?"

"Get up! You have to help us find Yeast People."

I clap my hands. "Okay!"

"Yeast People! Where are you?" Rosa picks up her cane. Mason gets his cane, too. "Yeast People! You can't hide! We're coming for you!" She sweeps her cane under the table. No Tom. She walks through the kitchen, searching. Searching.

"Hmm, where oh where is Tom?" I muse. He crawled in the direction of the living room. All the student apartments have the same basic layout, with an open kitchen adjacent to a living room, so I know what to expect. Stepping into the living room, I look around. The rectangular outline of a couch stands against one wall. No Tom. I approach an armchair in the middle of the room. No Tom. Next I peek behind the armchair. Nothing.

"Tom! We know you're here!" Scanning the room, I spy something in the far corner. I walk over and touch it—it's a chest of drawers. I probe behind it. Nothing.

I don't see any more furniture in the living room. Maybe he's hiding in the bedroom or bathroom? Retracing my steps, I walk through the living room again. Walking past the couch, I notice a large dark painting above the couch. Curious, I step closer. That's not a painting! That's Tom leaning against the corner, standing on the arm of the couch!

Covering my mouth, I dash over to the armchair and fall in laughing.

"Did you find him?" Rosa calls from the kitchen.

"Yes!"

Rosa and Mason bustle into the living room. "Where is he?" Rosa demands.

"Umm..." My first thought is: if I don't tell her, she'll chase me. My second thought is: if I help her, Tom will chase me.

My third thought is: if I move quietly enough, I can hide on top of that chest of drawers.

What should I do?

Rosa's question forces me to grapple with my role in this game. I have more usable vision than the other three, and Rosa knows this. Playing blind hide-and-seek with my eyes open gives me an unfair advantage. Providing Rosa with information I gained through sight would disrupt the structure of the game. It would let her skip finding Tom herself and skip using her nonvisual searching skills. In a word: cheating.

LCB instructors have warned us about the hierarchy of sight, a system where society privileges those who have more sight. Blind people sometimes internalize the hierarchy of sight, with those who are totally blind deferring to the partially sighted, and the partially sighted deferring to the fully sighted. Such classifications divide the blind community and contribute to our oppression. The training program has been teaching us to recognize and resist the oppressive system.

I don't want a blind world where the one-eyed man is automatically king.

Even though Rosa asked for my help, I decide to sit out the rest of the game. "He's here, somewhere." I blush, aware of how unhelpful that sounded. "Check every table, every chair, every corner!"

Rosa talks to Mason, then they spread out, exploring different parts of the living room. "Yeast People!" Rosa calls out. "Where are you, Yeast People?"

Mason approaches the couch.

I lean forward in my chair, holding my breath.

He bends over to touch the couch, scanning with one hand while the other holds his cane. He moves down the couch, touches another cushion, takes two steps, touches another cushion, then shuffles away.

I breathe out. He missed Tom. The game is still on!

Rosa, tapping her cane, approaches the couch. She tosses her cane on the floor and swipes both hands across the couch. She finds the couch seats empty.

I glance over at the tall figure standing on the couch and burst into delighted laughter. Convulsive, full body laughs. His hiding spot is creative, clever, brilliant! Blind hide-and-seek beats sighted hide-and-seek. It's more challenging, more exciting, more fun. We could give sighted people sleepshades and teach it to them.

Tom is educated, responsible, has a job, and still finds time in his life to play. When I'm fifty years old, I hope to be light-hearted enough to leap into a game of hide-and-seek.

"Haben, come here," Rosa orders.

I walk over to the front door where she and Mason are standing. "Here."

"It's time to go. We're leaving now. Bye, Yeast People!" She opens the front door, stomps her cane several times, then listens.

I bite my lip, determined to keep quiet.

We wait about three minutes, until Rosa closes the door. "He's not here," she tells Mason.

"He is here! He's being very sneaky. Check every chair, every table, every corner." I blush, feeling guilty for getting involved.

Mason and Rosa search through the apartment again. I sink

back into the armchair. Rosa notices the chair and starts patting it down.

"It's me! It's Haben!"

She pats my knee. "Sorry, baby." She turns away from the armchair and heads to the couch. "Yeast People! Oh, Yeast People!" She runs her hands over the first couch cushion, then picks it up and checks underneath. She inspects the corresponding back cushion, too. She methodically scrutinizes each cushion, all the way down the couch.

Rosa screams.

Tom jumps off the couch. Rosa smacks his legs with her cane. "Yeast People! I found you!" She whacks him again.

"It took you forever to find me." Tom sits down on the couch.

"You're not supposed to stand on furniture!" Rosa smacks him again.

Mason joins them on the couch, and all three talk over one another.

"Hey, I can't hear you guys." I pull my chair closer.

Tom raises his voice. "Quiet, Rosa! Haben can't hear me."

"Good!" she retorts. "All you say is lies."

"As I was saying," Tom clears his throat. "The best place to hide is in unexpected places. People always check the couch seats, but no one ever checks the arms. You have to go where people least expect."

"That was awesome," I tell him. "And hilarious. But what's the point? It's not like we can do anything with that information."

"My point... if you need to hide from your blind instructors tomorrow, now you know what to do."

I gasp, then break into giggles.

"Haben, there doesn't have to be a point to everything. We're just having fun. If you want to be serious, the skills we use in games can be transferred to work. Hide-and-seek develops searching skills, orientation skills, listening skills. Rosa, you could have listened more."

"You were too quiet!" she counters.

"The more you practice, the more sounds you can pick up. Like breathing. I think all blind kids should play hide-and-seek," he says.

"And blind adults," I add.

Tom chuckles. "Oh, yes!"

A few minutes later we exchange goodbyes. Rosa, Mason, and I head to our separate apartments.

I'm so glad I decided to step back and let Rosa find Tom on her own. She deserved to experience the thrill of discovery. Growing up as a blind person in a sighted world, there have been many instances where well-meaning sighted people denied me that thrill. We all need to get better at knowing when to help and when to back off and say, "Check every corner."

Chapter Fifteen

A Positive Blindness Philosophy

Ruston, Louisiana. Summer 2006.

Pam, the director of LCB, leads consciousness-raising seminars that examine the state of blindness in society. The dominant culture promotes ableism, the idea that people with disabilities are inferior to the nondisabled. Assumptions like: disability is a tragedy; disabled people are unteachable; it's better to be dead than disabled. LCB teaches students to resist these ableist assumptions. After identifying and removing them, people can begin to lay the groundwork for a positive philosophy based on the idea that blindness is nothing more than a lack of sight.

A group of us students form a circle in the library, facing Pam. She has a microphone clipped to her shirt that is wirelessly transmitting to my receiver and headphones, part of an assistive listening system I plan to use in college.

"I'm going to read a story," Pam tells us. "It's called *A Man Who Had No Eyes*, by MacKinlay Kantor."

Pam begins reading from a braille page on her lap. In the story, a blind beggar approaches a gentleman. The beggar presses a cigarette lighter in the gentleman's hand, asking for a dollar. The gentleman says he doesn't smoke, but the beggar just wheedles until he gets a dollar. The beggar senses that the gentleman has more money, so he tells the tale of how he lost his sight at a factory explosion, dramatizing and embellishing details. Then the gentleman reveals that he worked at that factory, too, and was there with the beggar during the explosion.

"The blind man stood for a long time, swallowing hoarsely. He gulped: 'Parsons. By God. By God! I thought you—' and then he screamed fiendishly: 'YES. MAYBE SO. MAYBE SO. BUT I'M BLIND! I'M BLIND, AND YOU'VE BEEN STANDING HERE LETTING ME SPOUT TO YOU, AND LAUGHING AT ME EVERY MINUTE! I'M BLIND.'

"People in the street turned to stare at him.

"'YOU GOT AWAY, BUT I'M BLIND! DO YOU HEAR?'

"'Well,' said Mr. Parsons, 'don't make such a row about it, Markwardt...So am I.'"

The room falls quiet.

"Haben." Pam turns her attention to me. "I'd like you to share your thoughts on the story with us."

"I love it! Imagine the shock and surprise of the beggar when he discovers Parsons is blind, too. The beggar assumed that if someone has money, then they're sighted."

"Thanks, Haben. The image of the blind beggar is so ingrained in our culture that people can barely imagine a successful blind person. Right? The story has a punch to it because most people can understand the shock of discovering a successful person is blind. Hopefully, sometime in the future we'll have so many stories of successful blind people that society will no longer be surprised by our success. Our culture will change, and society will get rid of the old assumptions. We need all of you to keep changing what it means to be blind."

Here at LCB, I'm surrounded by people who understand that blindness is just limited eyesight. With the right tools and training, blind people can compete as equals with sighted peers. Places like LCB exist to help blind people gain the tools and training to succeed. Sadly, our views on blindness are a minority view outside of these walls. There's a good chance a lot of the people I will meet in college next week will hold the same views as that blind beggar in the story. Part of me wishes I could stay here, but then I remember the mandatory cooking classes.

Somehow, someway, I'm going to create a community of people who believe that disability itself is not a barrier; the biggest barriers are social, physical, and digital. I hope I have the strength and skills to teach LCB's lessons to the world.

But first, college.

Chapter Sixteen

I Don't Believe Fairy Tales, Except This One

Portland, Oregon. Fall 2006.

Lewis & Clark College has a beautiful campus on the outskirts of Portland, Oregon. Dale, the director of disability services, gave me the grand tour during orientation. She showed me the shelf inside the Student Support Services office where all my braille texts wait for me to read them. She led me through the different entrances to the Templeton Campus Center: through the glass doors across the street from my residence hall, up the long flight of stairs by the mail room, across the large lawn by the Trail Room, and another entrance along a path that goes over a brook and through the woods. Thanks to the thorough tour with Dale, I now feel comfortable navigating campus on my own.

In fact, this evening I will join three students on an off-campus adventure. Two of the students and I are waiting just outside our residence hall. We live in Akin, a small two-story building that hosts a community of students who value diversity.

Living in Akin should increase my chances of meeting disability-positive people. Friendships take time, but my roommate already seems like a potential new friend. Carrie loves dancing, traveling, and eating chocolate—we're a perfect match!

Carrie runs over. "Okay, I'm ready. Wait. Haben, can I talk to you a moment?"

"Sure." I follow her as she moves away from the group.

Carrie stops in front of the stairs to our building. "We're going off campus."

"I know."

"We're not taking the bus. We're taking a back trail."

"Okay."

"It's a steep trail. I wouldn't want you to get hurt."

I smile. "Really, I'll be fine. I've done a lot of hiking. I'm able to feel the trail through my cane, and my cane will alert me to rocks and stuff."

"I don't think it's a good idea. There's a chance it could be a bit slippery. I really don't want you to get hurt. If anything happened to you, I would feel responsible."

I give her a serious look. "You're not responsible for me. If anything happens to me, it won't be your fault. Does that make sense?"

"I would still feel responsible. I'd never forgive myself. That's just how I am. Please, it would make me feel better if you didn't come with us."

Her words stab my fragile first-year heart. I pull my shoulders back. "I understand."

"Thank you! I'll see you later." With that, she runs back to the group, and they take off into the night.

My cane clangs against the stairs into Akin. I stomp down the hall to my room, slamming the door on the cold, callous, cruel college world. How am I supposed to live with her? My stomach churns at the thought of spending a whole year with someone who thinks I'm incompetent. How do I resist ableism in my own room?

I fall on my bed, weighed down by grief. Her condescension shattered my dream of having a college roommate who was also my best friend. I don't know how to fill that hole, now. Carrie's bed stands seven feet from me, her desk across from mine. We could pretend these are two rooms on either side of an invisible line. Will we live in a constant state of tension, fighting over one issue after another? Or will we live out separate lives, polite and indifferent whenever we're forced to interact? It'll be lonely. Awkward. Exhausting. It'll be a constant reminder that there will always be people in this world who believe I'm incompetent. Or just don't like me, period.

I massage my temples, trying to numb the pain. A memory flashes through my mind, the broad strokes of a fairy tale a friend shared long ago.

Sofia plopped down next to her grandmother with a sigh. "Every single one has issues. I'll never find the perfect guy."

"I've tried to tell you." The grandmother pulled down jasmine tea from a shelf.

"If you want to find your perfect match, you must first become your perfect self."

Sofia gazed at her grandmother with a furrowed brow.

The grandmother prepared tea, then began to explain how:

"I'll arrange dinners for you to practice listening, being vulnerable, and sharing your lovely wit.

"We'll reflect on the date and repeat the process each week, until one feels like the perfect fit."

Sweat formed on Sofia's face. She cleared it with a quick swipe.

"Grandma, I love you, but...you don't know my type."

"That's my point!" The grandmother waved a frustrated hand in the air.

"You need to stop judging guys on everything from their shoes to their hair."

Reaching for her tea, Sofia inhaled the warm, heavenly smell.

She sipped from the steaming cup. "Sure...Might as well."

Sofia met local men and foreign men.

Fishermen and firemen.

Her eyelids drooped as a guy described the best soil to plant a seed in.

She stifled a yawn as a man droned on about the tax system in Sweden.

Through practice and reflection, her listening skills grew.

As she voiced her plans and dreams, her confidence soared, too.

She shared her thoughts on bridge design with an investor from Taipei.

She educated a businessman on the importance of equal pay.

Her stories delighted her dinner partners and their waitstaff.

During one lively dinner, she even got a lawyer to laugh!

At the thirty-ninth dinner, she felt a jolt of elation.
She asked the guy out again, continuing their flirtation.
They built a relationship, not on diamonds and dollar bills,
But on plates of savory food, and strong interpersonal skills.

The story makes me smile and shake my head. It's a silly story, but it carries a bit of wisdom. If Sofia's strategy works for romantic relationships, then it must work for friendships, too.

Cane in hand, I step outside my room and close the door. The door has blue and white stripes with a yellow sun in the corner. It's the flag of Uruguay. All the rooms in this residence hall have a flag on the door, giving Akin a certain warmth. I squint at the colorful doors as I walk by, trying to identify the flags.

Another door opens down the hall. A person steps out.

"Hi, I'm Haben." I switch my cane to my left hand and offer the person my right. The hand is large. "What's your name?"

"Ed."

"Nice to meet you, Ed."

"Nice to meet you, too."

"Want to hang out? We could play a card game."

"Maybe later."

"Okay, just let me know. I'm in Uruguay." I gesture behind me. "That's the door with blue stripes and a yellow sun in the corner. Room 101."

"Got it." Ed turns and walks down the hall.

My search through the hall for a new friend fails, but my optimism doesn't waver. There are still a lot of people to meet—at least one of them will resonate with me.

Over the next four weeks I approach lots of people. I practice listening, being compassionate, and displaying my sense of humor. My ability to laugh at myself comes in handy when people do the awkward "Umm, we've already met" dance.

Many students meet at the cafeteria. It's called the Bon, pronounced "Bone," because the company Bon Appetit runs it. The large rectangular room has three walls with panoramic windows, showcasing Portland's rain. The fourth wall has several food stations. Sighted students browse the print menu, and then go to their station of choice. I can't read the menu since it's not available in an accessible format.

A long line of students stand in front of station one. Guessing it might be something good, I join the line. Cooking smells swirl around the room, blending into that vague cafeteria food scent. Unlike today's food, some foods have aromas that refuse to mix, pumping their molecules through the airwaves with unabashed pride. Pancakes. French fries. Pizza. They perform a nonstop chorus of, "Come eat us!"

After fifteen minutes in line, I finally reach the counter. "What do you have here?" I ask the server. The background noise of the cafeteria drowns out the response. "What?" I lean over the counter. "Sorry, I'm still not hearing that." The person shouts inaudible words. Tired and hungry, I accept a plate from the server.

The voices of hundreds of students bouncing off the walls form a persistent roar that increases as I enter the seating area—rows of round tables surrounded by hungry students. I squint at the seats near me as I squeeze through the crowded aisles. Finally, an empty chair—I touch the back of it and verify that it really is empty.

The seats on either side of me have people. Smiling, I turn to the person on my left. "Hi, I'm Haben. What's your name?"

Mumble, mumble, mumble.

"I don't hear very well, especially in noisy places. Could you say your name again?" I lean to the left, hoping to catch it this time.

"Pam."

"Pam?"

Louder this time. "Anne."

"Anne? How's your lunch?"

Her face turned toward me suggests she has offered a response to my question. The roar of chatter around us swallows up her words. The noise forms a glass wall between us. I'm on one side, and Anne and everyone else is on the other.

The grandmother marked listening as the first important skill to master, and this environment makes that impossible. The world shrinks to just the plate in front of me as I realize I won't form any friendships here.

Picking up my fork, I touch the tip to different areas of the plate, analyzing the textures. The fork pokes at meat on a bone. My shoulders sag. I wanted a vegetarian meal. I continue the investigation. On the right, something soft. I scoop up a tiny portion and take a bite. Mashed potatoes. I take another bite. The smooth potatoes melt in my mouth. Not bad.

I glance over in the direction of the food stations. Another station probably has something delicious. Saag paneer with jasmine rice. Pennini with smoked Gouda cheese. Soul-filling food and friendships, it's all over there, beyond the glass wall.

"Nice meeting you," I mumble in Anne's direction as I leave.

*   *   *

Unlike the cafeteria, the disability office provides information in accessible formats. I first met Dale and her colleagues Rebecca and Barbara back in April. I'm their first braille reader, and that didn't faze them one bit. They purchased a braille embosser, purchased braille translation software, and then spent the summer learning how to produce braille. They're not afraid of the unknown; they learn, explore, and discover for the sake of their students and the betterment of themselves. They represent the pioneering spirit Lewis & Clark College celebrates.

Rebecca is the reading specialist, so she expanded her talents to include braille. After securing syllabi from all my professors, she began ordering books in braille from the National Braille and Talking Book Library, and Bookshare. When a book is not available, she asks publishers for a digital copy of the book so she can emboss it in braille herself. The braille embosser is a large printer that punches dots into thick braille paper. It sounds like a jackhammer, so Rebecca stationed the machine in a large closet.

"Perfect timing!" Rebecca hands me a braille volume. "I just finished printing this. Thomas threw a tantrum this morning and I had to put him in time-out."

I give her a confused look. "Who's Thomas?"

"The braille embosser. I spend so much time with it, I started calling him Thomas."

I smile. "I like that. I hope Thomas behaves."

"He better. Or I'll have a word with his maker."

Rebecca, Barb, and Dale remove any access barriers in my

classes, allowing me to devote my time to studying. Other colleges force blind students to sacrifice their precious study hours to convert course materials themselves. The struggle of juggling both making materials accessible and learning the course materials causes many blind students to fall behind. While I exhaust myself to excel, logging numerous hours in the library, the college's dedicated accessibility team also contributes to my success.

That evening, I spot an empty table in the Bon. It calls to me. Sit here! Sit here! You won't have to exhaust yourself trying to connect with people you can't hear. Think of your poor ears. Think of the peacefulness of sitting here!

The corner location creates a tranquil refuge. A wall behind me and another to my right absorb the background noise. Even the food tastes better here. The flavors in this pizza have my full attention now that I don't have to strain to hear.

Someone pauses at my table. I continue eating. The person remains standing there, as if waiting. "Did you say something?"

"Can I sit here?"

"Sure." I take another bite of pizza.

He sets his tray on the table and sits down across from me. Mumble, mumble, mumble.

"I'm pretty Deaf. It helps if you talk louder and try to talk slowly and clearly."

"Is this better?"

"Yeah. I'll still miss stuff now and then. What did you say?"

"I was asking your name."

"Oh!" I laugh. "My name is Haben. What's yours?"

"Justin. I'm a senior studying history."

"I'm a first-year. I don't know what I'll major in. Maybe computer science, maybe international affairs...I'm going to take a few different classes to figure out what I want to do."

"That's smart. Explore different subjects until you find a topic you love so much you'll voluntarily lock yourself up in the library. By the way, how's the pizza?"

"It's actually pretty good."

"Yeah, that looks good. I'm going to grab some." He heads to the food stations. A few minutes later he comes back carrying two plates.

"What did you get?"

"I got some of that pizza. I also picked up a brownie. It was calling me when I walked by and I had to go back for it."

I gasp. "I didn't know they had those." I raise my cane from under the table. "I'll be right back."

I march over to the dessert station and seize a brownie from under the glass wall. My cane clears the way as I carry the prize back to the table.

"Whoa, I had no idea you were blind," Justin says as I sit down. "Not that it's a big deal—I just didn't know until you picked up the cane."

"That's funny. Most people here know." My mood dips as I consider all the images of blindness that might be running through his head. I brace myself for offensive, ableist comments. "Blindness is actually just the lack of sight. With the right tools and training, blind people can do just about anything. Like, I travel, rock climb, and volunteer in my community. I just use alternative techniques."

"Yeah, I figured. My mom is a special ed teacher."

My eyes widen in surprise. Meeting new people often involves exorcising the specter of ableism. Meeting someone who has a background in disability feels miraculous. "That's awesome. What kind of disabilities do your mom's students have?"

"Mostly learning disabilities. Hey! How's it going?"

I stare at Justin, confused. A moment later another person joins our table. Mumble, mumble, mumble. The two chatter away. I start eating my brownie.

"Haben, this is Gordon. Gordon, this is Haben."

"Hi." I shake Gordon's hand.

"Can you say your name again?"

"Ha-ben."

Mumble, mumble.

"I'm Deaf. It helps if you talk louder, and speak slowly and clearly."

Gordon increases his volume. "I've never heard that name before. Where is your family from?"

"My family is from Eritrea, a country in northeast Africa. Haben is a name in Tigrinya, the native language of Eritrea."

"What does *Haben* mean in Tigrinya?"

My breath catches in my throat. Wow, he's genuinely listening to me. Most people tune out after hearing unfamiliar names like Tigrinya and Eritrea. Feeling overwhelmed, they change the subject. This guy doesn't run from the unknown, though. "Eritrea gained independence in 1993 after a thirty-year war with its large neighbor Ethiopia. My parents named me after our culture's sense of pride in standing up for freedom and independence. *Haben* in Tigrinya means pride."

"That's fascinating. I'll have to read up on Eritrea."

Mumble, mumble. Justin and Gordon fall into a conversation, and the familiar glass wall settles between us.

I finish the brownie. "What are you two talking about?"

"Gordon plans to major in history, so he was asking me about professors," Justin says.

"I was asking Justin about Professor Hillyer's teaching style."

"What does he teach?" I ask.

"Professor Hillyer is a woman," Gordon says.

I blush, embarrassed. Although, I'm secretly glad he corrected me. Many people just overlook the mistakes of people with disabilities, assuming we're too fragile. "What does she teach?"

"She has a Civil War history class that I'm considering." Gordon slips back into inaudible conversation with Justin. The hum of background noise has risen to a roar, and the glass wall slides up again.

I stand up. "It's too loud in here. I'm going to head out now."

"I'm actually done, too." Justin gets to his feet, and Gordon follows.

We slide our trays onto the dish racks in the corner of the Bon, then head for the exit. As I walk outside I observe Justin and Gordon still walking beside me. We seem to be leaving together, but it's probably just a coincidence. My expectations sank to the bottom of the sea after what happened with Carrie.

A soothing silence envelopes us as we step out on the sidewalk. I breathe in the cool autumn air. Then my nose wrinkles at a whiff of cigarette smoke.

The silence stretches into awkwardness. I look from Justin

to Gordon wondering if I should bid them farewell. Then I remember Sofia and her grandmother. The cafeteria environment limits my ability to listen to people, but out here...

"I live in Akin." I point to the short building in front of us.

"Isn't that the international dorm?" Gordon asks.

"Multicultural. If you're curious, I can give you a tour."

"Sure. Justin?"

"Yeah, sure." He tosses something on the ground and stomps on it with his shoe.

My cane taps the street. "Okay, follow me."

I show them the Akin living room with its comfy couches, panoramic windows, and a piano. Adjacent to the living room is a small kitchen where every week someone burns food, setting off the fire alarm. I show them the hallways with their world flags. "Now for the basement!" I guide them down a staircase, down a dark hallway, and into a dark room. My hand finds the light switch and flicks it on.

"Cool!" Justin steps into the game room. "Let's play pool. I'm not very good at it, but it's fun." He hops around the table clearing it of cue sticks and removing balls from pockets.

"How does the game work exactly?" My mind tugs at faint memories of hitting pool balls with my sister.

Gordon steps up to the table. "I think you try to hit the white ball so it pushes other balls into pockets."

Justin holds up a cue stick. "Yeah, something like that. Whoever sinks the most balls wins. I'll go first." He adjusts his aim, then fires off a shot.

Pow! Balls clatter around the table.

I approach the table. "Did any go in?"

"Two went in. Here," Justin hands me a cue stick. It feels familiar, like a cousin of the white cane. "Want to go next?"

After weeks of exclusion, a simple gesture of inclusion leaves me dizzy. "Sure ... Where's the white ball?"

He points to the left side of the table. I walk over, peering down at the green table. Three balls shimmer in my field of vision. My eyes can't pinpoint their exact location, just their general area on the left side of the table. I extend a hand to determine their exact positions.

"Haben's cheating!" Gordon points at my hand.

"I'm not moving them, just feeling their location." I continue touching the balls.

"I know. I'm just messing with you."

I straighten up and face him, bouncing the cue stick on my palm. "That's not your smartest move, messing with someone holding a stick."

"Watch out, Gordon!" Justin howls with laughter.

"I'm watching you." Gordon backs away from the table.

I verify the position of the balls one last time, then take aim at the white ball. Pow! Balls careen around the table. I start examining the pockets. "Did any go in?"

"You got one," Justin says.

"Wow." The small victory fuels my competitive side. I continue using my tactile techniques through the rest of the game. At the end, I'm in first, then Justin, then Gordon.

Delighted, I raise my cane in the air. "Blind girl wins!"

"Did you say, 'Black girl wins?'" Justin asks.

"That works, too!" I laugh. "I actually said, 'Blind girl wins.' Justin, how do you identify?"

"Sighted, although I wear glasses."

I make a face. "Actually—"

"I know what you meant. I'm white. My mom is from Connecticut and my dad is from Georgia."

"So you're half southerner and half Yankee."

Justin laughs. "Exactly, though I'm mostly a northerner. I grew up in Connecticut."

"And you, Gordon?"

"White. I grew up in Southeast Alaska."

"Really?" I adopt a teasing tone. "Did you live in an igloo?"

"No! My parents have a house, a modern house. No one lives in igloos."

I stifle a laugh. "All right, no igloos. Did you have huskies driving you around on sleds?"

"Good God, no. We don't do dog sledding. My parents do have a Samoyed, a big fluffy dog with pointy ears, kind of like a husky. Why? What is this?"

I grin. "It's payback for fussing every time I touched the pool balls."

"Fine, I'll pretend I don't know you were cheating."

"That was *not* cheating!" I sigh. "You know, I could keep making the Alaskan jokes."

"I need to go get some homework done." Justin drops his cue stick on the table. "But I'll also think of some Alaskan jokes."

"Hey! I thought you were on my side." Gordon hoists his backpack onto his shoulders.

"You rock, Justin!" I lead the way upstairs. "Hey Gordon, what do Alaskans read?"

Justin asks, "They can read?"

"Yeah, they read brrrrraille!"

Gordon lets out a dramatic sigh.

When Justin or Gordon see me in the Bon, they walk right up to me and tell me where they're sitting in the large room. Students never invited me to their tables in my K–12 cafeterias. Having people ask me to sit with them feels strange and wonderful, like a desert-dweller discovering a reliable source of water.

The three of us try to arrive early for meals, when the noise level is at its lowest. Tables next to walls have superior acoustics. Capturing one of these, especially a corner table, feels like a little victory.

The Bon doesn't serve Eritrean or Ethiopian food, and Justin and Gordon have never tried it. Gordon and I are looking up restaurants from the campus center's computer room. Gordon stares into a monitor as he looks up the route to the Blue Nile, an Ethiopian restaurant in Portland.

He disappears into the visual world of the computer while I sit by, waiting, seemingly forever. Time slows to an unbearable crawl as he silently interacts with the inaccessible screen—another glass wall. I debate going to the accessible computer in my room and just looking up the route myself.

I drum my fingers on the table. "Are you looking up how to get to Mexico?"

His eyes stay fixed on the screen. "This map only shows North America."

"Mexico is in North America."

"No, it's in South America."

I burst out laughing. "Mexico is in North America. Look it up!"

"What?" He starts furiously typing.

My rib cage shakes with laughter. My whole body, even my chair, vibrates with the belly-laughs that roll over me like waves. They pause long enough for me to ask, "Where did you go to school, Alaska?"

"Okay, you're right. It's North America."

"Told you!" I burst into another round of chair-shaking hysterics.

"Oh, stop that! At least I don't assume a professor's a man or something dumb like that."

The memory of my sexist comment stifles my mirth.

A woman starts shouting behind us. "Don't call her that! Haben is not dumb! She's intelligent, and you need to be nice to her!"

My body stiffens as my mind tries to label the emotion coursing through my veins. Fear? Anger? Despair?

Navigating ableist situations is like traversing the muckiest mud pit. Ableism runs so deep in our society that most ableists don't recognize their actions as ableist. They coat ableism in sweetness, then expect applause for their "good" deeds. Attempts to explain the ableism behind the "good deeds" get brushed aside as sensitive, angry, and ungrateful.

My nerves jangle as I clear my throat. "We're just joking around. You don't need to speak for me."

The woman storms out of the room.

"Who was that?" I whisper.

"That girl who hangs out with Carrie."

"Anika."

"Yeah. She and Carrie keep talking down to you and it's super condescending."

"You noticed!" A warm, summery feeling sweeps over me. I feel weightless, like the sensation on the high point of a swing. "I thought no one else noticed. It always feels like they're talking down to me, and everyone else calls it 'being nice.'"

A heady mix of astonishment and relief pulse through me. He gets it. He really, truly gets it. I no longer have to face ableism alone.

Chapter Seventeen

Ableism and the Art of Blind PB&J

Oakland, California. Fall 2006.

Lewis & Clark closes for Thanksgiving weekend, so I fly down to Oakland to celebrate with my family. We feast on Eritrean food: spicy sautéed spinach, spicy chickpea curry, spicy potatoes and carrots, and all of it served with injera, the spongy flatbread that cradles the delicious flavors. We eat Eritrean food on Thanksgiving Day, on Black Friday, and now on Saturday we're having another party at my parents' house, with yet more Eritrean food.

As much as I don't want to, I need to start getting ready for my trip back to Portland. "I'm going to pack sandwiches for my flight tomorrow," I tell Saba.

"Okay. Don't let Yafet see you," she warns.

Yafet, my little cousin, expresses his love by demanding to have whatever my sister TT and I have. If he sees TT eating cake, he insists on having more cake—even if he's already had four slices. If he sees me eating a banana, he orders me to get him another banana, even when he is completely full. He makes himself sick trying to have what we have. If I tell him he's had enough, he throws a tantrum that leaves our parents begging us to give him what he wants. The clever kid always gets his way.

I slip into the kitchen. It's empty, thank goodness. I bring down a jar of peanut butter from the cabinet and retrieve strawberry jam from the refrigerator. Next, I place a plate on the counter, along with a knife. After tossing two slices of bread on the plate, I open the jar of peanut butter.

Yafet pops up beside me. My heart starts pounding. His head doesn't reach the counter, but his voice reverberates around the room. "What are you doing?"

"Making a PB&J," I mumble. "It's for my lunch tomorrow."

"Oh." He stands there watching. "Make me one," he orders. He pauses for a beat, then continues. "You know, if you don't make me one I'm just gonna tell Auntie Saba on you. She's gonna tell you to make me one, so you better just make me one."

He's right. The adults always take his side. If I want to escape being blackmailed by my little cousin, I need to get creative, and fast.

I keep a straight face as I ask, "Can a blind person make a peanut butter and jelly sandwich?"

He thinks for a second. "No."

I continue in a calm, neutral voice. "Am I blind?"

"Yes."

"Well, then, if a blind person can't make a PB&J, then I can't make you one, right?"

Yafet just stands there. He watches me make the sandwiches. I start closing the jars.

"Ugh!" He runs out of the kitchen screaming, "Auntie Saba! Haben said...Haben won't..." A minute later he dashes back. "Haben," he commands, "Auntie Saba says you have to make me a PB&J."

I raise an eyebrow. "You said a blind person can't make a PB&J. So how can I make you a PB&J?"

"But I saw you!" he wails.

His personal observations contradict the "truth" he learned from society that all blind people are incompetent. Contradictory beliefs create stress, so people drop one to create harmony. This is Cognitive Dissonance Theory. Most people choose to accept ableism, because rejecting it—going against the dominant narrative—would take more conscious effort. I want Yafet to reject ableism. If he says that a blind person can make a PB&J, then I'll make him one.

"So you saw me make a PB&J? That's interesting. Now let's consider that for a second—does that mean that a blind person can make a PB&J?"

He thinks for a bit. "No."

"I can't make you a sandwich, then. Sorry."

He stomps his feet and stalks out of the kitchen.

Yafet came very close to accepting that blind people can in fact make PB&Js. I'm confident that one day, when he's older, he'll have the courage to reject ableism in favor of what he actually observes.

Yes, I can make a PB&J, but come on—at least say *please*.

Chapter Eighteen

Never, Ever, Run from a Bear

Portland, Oregon. Fall 2006.

I hold out a Tupperware container to Justin and Gordon. "My mom made this over Thanksgiving. *Kitcha fitfit* is shredded flat bread sautéed in butter and *berbere*, a fiery Eritrean spice."

They reach in and take a piece. The savory scents of Eritrean spiced butter and *berbere* waft through the small room. The Akin study room has a blue couch along one wall, two blue armchairs, and a tall shelf full of books and games. Here, we can have conversations without interfering background noise.

"It's really spicy," Justin says, coughing a little. "I can handle spice better than most people, but this is really spicy."

I raise an eyebrow. "Most people? You mean most Americans. This hardly counts as spicy to Eritreans."

"That's true." Justin reaches in for more. "In a way, it's kind of like the fry bread at the Bon today, except with this *berbere* spice."

My stomach sinks. "They had fry bread today?"

"Yeah, at lunch. Isn't there a way for you to get the menus?" Gordon asks.

"It's not in braille or anything, so I've just been trying to guess where the interesting stuff is based on the lines."

Justin takes some more *kitcha*. "Why don't you get a plate from every station, taste a bite from each plate, then eat the good stuff?"

I frown. "That would waste a lot of food. Plus, that would mean spending my whole lunch period in long lines being bored, tired, and hungry."

"Next you're going to ask her if she can just sniff the stations," Gordon says.

I pull the container away from them. "Are you going to ask me that, Justin? Or you?" I give Gordon a warning look.

"Your sense of smell is actually better than mine," Justin says. "Not because you're blind, but because I smoke like a chimney."

"Mhm." I pointedly stare at Gordon.

"Can I have more *kitcha fitfit*?" he asks.

"No."

"I was joking. I don't think being blind automatically gives someone a superior sense of smell," Gordon says. "Besides, the cafeteria is constantly cooking multiple things at the same time, and all the stations are right next to one another. It all blends together."

I push the container back toward them. "Good answer. I was worried you couldn't tell the difference between humans and huskies."

Justin leans in. "He was chasing me the other day and I had to explain to him that I'm not a moose."

Emperor Haile Selassie honored my grandfather Kidane Adgoy for his efforts to free Ethiopia and Eritrea from Italian colonization. My grandfather bows slightly, his gaze respectfully downcast, as he reaches out a hand to receive a small case from the emperor. The emperor and my grandfather are both wearing dark gray suits and solemn expressions. In the background stand eight men in similar dark suits, and two photographers using large press cameras with attached flashbulbs. *Copyright Kidane Family Collection.*

One of my favorite pastimes is getting my mother, Saba, to laugh. She's standing outside my father's home in Addis Ababa with one of her dazzling smiles. She has a translucent gray scarf around her shoulders, and her sunglasses sparkle in the sun. Behind her is a paved path lined with vibrant green shrubbery and red flowers. *Copyright Girma Family Collection.*

Grandmother Awiye smiles warmly as she faces the camera. A white scarf called a *netsela* is draped around her head and shoulders. *Copyright Girma Family Collection.*

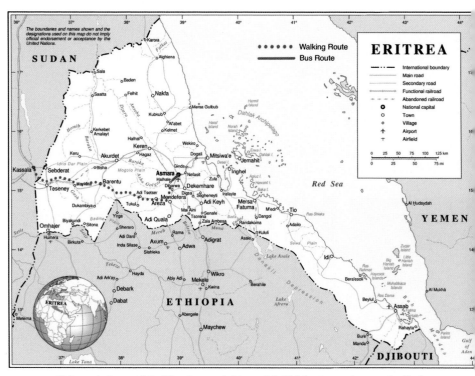

Eritrea is located in Northeast Africa with Ethiopia to the south, Sudan to the north, the Red Sea along the northeast, and Djibouti to the east. My mother rode a bus from Asmara to a nearby village called Halhale, then walked about 320 km (203 miles) west to Kassala, Sudan. She walked barefoot for most of the three-week trip. This map is derived from a map created by the United Nations.

Seven-year-old me clung to my dad like Velcro, determined to do whatever he did. In our yard in Oakland he enjoyed lounging on a bed he built himself, taking in the sun while reading one of his books. In this photo he's lying on his stomach with a thick book open in front of him. I'm fast asleep on his back, and he's looking over his shoulder wondering whether he should keep reading with the weight of a sleeping child on his back, or risk waking me up. *Copyright Girma Family Collection.*

The way Yafet embraces lotion is exactly how he embraces life. My four-year-old cousin's face is slathered in it, with globs of lotion all over his face, hands, and pajamas. *Copyright Gebreyesus Family Photo.*

An enormous iceberg, about thirty feet tall, fills most of this photo. It's a pale, almost-white blue, with a hint of yellow. I stand beside the iceberg on Mendenhall Lake, touching it with a gloved hand. This is not the iceberg we climbed. *Copyright Girma Family Collection.*

Dean Martha Minow hands me a diploma as I cross the stage at Harvard Law School's graduation ceremony. Dean Minow and I are both wearing academic regalia. My guide dog Maxine is wearing a fabulous fur coat. *Copyright Girma Family Collection.*

President Barack Obama stands by a tall table as he types with all his fingers. I'm reading his words as they appear on my braille computer, positioned on the other side of the table. Vice President Joe Biden and Valerie Jarrett are also standing in the Blue Room observing our conversation. *Photo by The White House / Pete Souza.*

President Barack Obama has his arm around my shoulder as he guides me through the Green Room. I'm holding my braille computer as we walk, and Vice President Joe Biden is right behind us. *Photo by The White House / Pete Souza.*

A powerful speech inspires audiences to take action. Here I'm speaking from the Summit at Sea stage, surrounded by glowing purple and orange coral structures. *Photo by Summit / Ian Rowan*

My sister TT, in her twenties now, stands on top of a hill with her arms outstretched triumphantly, the city of San Francisco behind her. She's wearing jeans, a colorful shirt, tinted black-framed glasses, and a big smile. *Copyright Girma Family Collection.*

My guide dog Maxine and I traveled all over the country to give talks on disability rights and inclusion. In this photo I'm kneeling beside Maxine in front of the University of Kansas bell tower. Maxine looks up at me, with her paw on my arm, as I gently explain, "We're not in California anymore." *Copyright Girma Family Collection*

Left, right, forward, and canter—communicating with a horse reminds me of working with a guide dog. In this photo I'm riding a tan-colored horse, holding the reins and smiling. Behind me are green rolling hills. *Copyright Girma Family Collection*

I love stand-up paddling, especially in warm water. I'm wearing a lifejacket and standing on a SUP board, paddle extended in front of me as I cross Kealakekua Bay. The water of the bay is a bit choppy, and in the distance are misty green hills. *Copyright Girma Family Collection*

My dear friends April and Brian Wilson gifted me with the honor of officiating their wedding. Brian, wearing his U.S. Navy uniform, stands at the altar gazing adoringly at April. She holds a bouquet of cream, pink, and orange flowers that complement her gorgeous blush pink dress. My hands read from my braille computer, placed on the altar between us, as I help them celebrate their love. The tranquil waters of the bay stretch out behind us. *Photo by Ryan Greenleaf*

I hold up a hand to Justin and we high five.

Gordon crosses his arms. "You people from the Lower 48 are all the same. You think Alaska is just moose and igloos. You probably think it's moose in igloos."

I collapse into a fit of giggles. "By the way, it's *forty-nine*! You forgot Hawaii."

"She's right," Justin says. "Hawaii is also geographically lower than Alaska. Why don't Alaskans say Lower 49 when referring to the rest of the United States?"

"I'm not sure..." Gordon munches *kitcha fitfit*. "I think it just refers to the mainland United States. My grandmother actually has a flag with forty-nine stars. It's one of the very few made after Alaska became a state and before Hawaii became a state."

"Cool! I'd love to see that flag," Justin says.

I reach for some *kitcha*. "I think I'll talk to the Bon about the menus."

The next day, Gordon and I head to the Bon Appetit office, located in the Templeton Campus Center.

I see someone standing by the door. "Hi, I'm looking for Claude," I tell them. Claude is the Bon manager, whom Dale introduced me to during orientation.

"He's at his desk," the guy says. I follow him to a desk in the corner.

"Can I help you?" the man behind the desk asks.

"Are you Claude?"

"Yes."

"My name is Haben. We met a while ago when Dale was

giving me a tour. I know you have a print menu up on the wall in the cafeteria, but I can't read it because I'm blind. Would you make the menu available in braille so blind people can also access it?"

"I'd be happy to read the menu to you. Or one of my colleagues could read it."

"I'm Deaf, too. Most of the time I can't hear what people are saying in the cafeteria because it's so loud. The noise won't matter if I have the menu in braille, though. Student Support Services has a braille embosser. If you send the menu in advance, they can braille it for me."

"Umm, I'm not sure if that would work. We sometimes have to change the menu at the last minute."

"Oh." I consider the alternatives. "You print out the menu for everyone, so you have it on computers, right? You could just copy and paste that menu into an email to me. I can access emails. My computer has a screenreader that converts text to digital braille."

"So just email the menu? We wouldn't need to do anything special to it?"

"Exactly. Just copy and paste the text into an email and I'll be able to read it."

"That seems pretty simple."

"Very simple. I'll give you my email address. Do you have a pen?"

Over the next few months, the Bon occasionally emails me the menus as Claude and I discussed. When the emails arrive, they're life-changing: I can go straight to the station serving a nice vegetarian meal and save myself both time and effort. More often, though, the emails don't come. On those days, I'm stuck choosing stations at random. I've stopped counting the number of times I've carried a plate of food, found a table, tried the food, and discovered an unpleasant surprise.

Once again, Gordon generously joins me as I raise the issue with the Bon Appetit office.

"The menus are not accessible," I tell Claude. "It's frustrating and stressful when I don't know what the stations are serving."

"I can get someone to read the menu to you," he offers.

"It's really hard to hear people in the cafeteria. When you email the menu, though, I can read it on my computer. Then I know exactly what each station is serving."

"We're all really busy here. We have hundreds of students. You can ask one of us to read the menu to you and we'd be happy to do that."

My frustration squeezes the air out of my lungs. "That's the thing—I can't *hear* people reading the menu. I'm Deaf. That's why I'm asking you to email me the menu."

"I'll talk to them." Claude starts walking out the door. "I need to get back to work." With that, he dismisses me.

When Gordon and I exit the building, a torrential rain pummels us.

I pull out an umbrella and hold it out to Gordon. "You should hold this since you're taller." He lifts it over the two of us, and we walk under the shelter through the pouring rain. "So, what do you think?" I ask.

"He was being a complete jerk."

Wind blows the rain at an angle, making our umbrella nearly useless. I pull my coat tighter around me. "He was nice the first time I talked to him, but now..."

"I hate the Bon. You're forced to pay for a meal plan if you live in the dorms, so even if you don't eat at the Bon you're still paying for it. And when you do eat there, it's crowded and they run out of food. The whole operation sucks."

"I don't like cooking, but I'd rather cook than eat at the Bon. I'm moving off campus as soon as they let me. I think the rule is that students have to live on campus for two years."

"I'd rather live off campus, too."

I tap the stairs with my cane as we begin our descent. "Remember when I challenged you and Justin to close your eyes and go down these stairs using a cane?"

"Justin was surprisingly good at it. You could sort of feel the tone of the different vibrations to sense what was around you."

"Mhm. That was fun."

Gordon stops in front of the library. "What are you going to do?"

I breathe a deep sigh, overwhelmed by it all. "I have two papers to write and an exam to study for. I shouldn't have to worry about my next meal." I tug on the umbrella. "I need to get to class. Thanks for going with me to Claude's office."

"Of course. You shouldn't have to deal with the Bon alone." He returns my umbrella, but it's his words—those precious words of solidarity—that shield me from the worst of the weather. Pulling myself away from the library, I trudge down the road to class in my rain-drenched shoes.

Maybe I should just accept inferior service at the cafeteria.

At least I have food. Around the world, millions of people struggle for food. When my mother was my age, she was a refugee in Sudan. Meanwhile, here I am attending an awesome American college with a full-tuition scholarship. Who am I to complain? Blind students at other colleges struggle to get access to course materials. By contrast, Lewis & Clark is doing a stellar job providing me all my course materials in braille. Claude's actions seem to say, "Go away, stop complaining, and be more appreciative of what you already have." Maybe he's right—maybe I should just be grateful.

That evening, the Bon doesn't email me a menu for dinner. Nor do they send a breakfast menu the following morning.

"Did they send you a lunch menu?" Gordon asks. We're in the Akin study room working on homework.

"Yeah, they sent the lunch menu." I raise my eyebrows. "After lunch."

"Wait, what? They sent you the lunch menu after lunch was over?"

I nod.

"Good God! It's 2007, sending emails is the easiest thing in the world. They're just being lazy."

"I've spent time in villages with limited resources. If I actually had to live with restricted access to food, I could. But the Bon has resources."

"This has to stop. Tell me how I can help."

I shrug. "I don't know. I think I'll email Claude and ask why the menus are so sporadic."

"Good. See what he says."

The menu situation continues through the weekend. On

Monday, Claude finally sends me a response. Gordon and I meet up at the library's assistive technology room that afternoon, and I show him the email:

Hi Haben,

I was not in the office before lunch, but I did get back after 3:00 and checked my email. It is likely what happened this time (and possibly in the past) is that even though our supervisor took the time to generate the email, they did not hit the send/receive button, so it sat in the outbox until I got back to check for new mail. I sincerely apologize for the inconvenience, it doesn't make much sense to take the time to type them up and not send them, I completely agree, so something must have come up.

We hope that you understand that this is something that we are trying to help you with, but you also need to understand that this is a service that we are not contracted to provide, and that unlike the college, we do not have people on staff to assist students with special needs. We will continue to do our best to help you, but it is not reasonable to have an expectation of us that we are not required to do (we never expressed that we could, or would, commit to this), and it is also unreasonable to expect that this assistance will come seamlessly. There will be meals that are missed, and there will be times that emails will arrive late. We are just not set up with the support staff to assist you personally in this matter—we work hard to meet the needs of over 1,000 students for every meal, so we hope you understand that we have a variety of concerns to address every service, and whenever possible we are giving you all of the help we can.

In speaking with several people associated with the college, we understand that this is frustrating for you, but we continue to recommend that you find someone at the school who can find you a regular and permanent solution.

Best,

Claude

"I can't stand that guy!" Gordon glances at the computer screen again. "He thinks the college has some magical disability solution so that he doesn't have to think about people's disabilities. He's the one with access to the menu, not Student Support Services."

"And Student Support Services told him to send me the menus, too. Dale even offered to braille them, but to do that she needs the Bon to send her the menus. I'm wondering..." I pause to collect my thoughts. "In the first part of the email he mentions typing. The menus are print-outs pinned to the wall by the door, right?"

"Exactly. It looks like they just type the menus in Microsoft

Word, print them out, and then hang them on the wall. There should be no reason for them to type the menu a second time. All they'd have to do is copy the text from the file and paste it into an email—and then actually hit send."

"Right." I half smile at that. "It's funny: the guy sends me an email saying he's not equipped to send emails!" I shake my head. "Lots of places are like this, refusing to accommodate people with disabilities because they don't want to think about disability. They treat serving people with disabilities as optional, charity work. They assume that only disability specialists can work with our 'special needs.' That term is so demeaning. The need to eat is a universal need, not a 'special' need."

"Aren't they required by law to serve students with disabilities?"

"I need to read up on the Americans with Disabilities Act. Can I have my computer back?" Gordon rolls his chair back over to his laptop, and I scoot my chair up to my computer. Over the next hour, I immerse myself in the details of the Americans with Disabilities Act (ADA). There are parts that are reassuring, and there are parts that are confusing. I begin drafting a response to Claude:

Hi Claude,

Bon Appetit has a legal obligation, under the Americans with Disabilities Act, to provide people with disabilities access to its services.

I have been asking Bon Appetit to make the menus accessible because I'm Deafblind and can't read the print menu or hear someone reading the menu in the noisy cafeteria. My computer has software that converts text on the screen to digital braille, so I would be able to access the menus if Bon Appetit emailed them to me.

Please understand that I'm not asking for a favor, I'm asking Bon Appetit to comply with the law. Under Title III of the ADA, places of public accommodation, like Bon Appetit, are prohibited from discriminating against people with disabilities. If Bon Appetit continues to deny me access, I'm going to take legal action.

Will Bon Appetit commit to making the menus accessible, consistently and professionally?

Sincerely,

Haben

After reviewing the email, I look up the email addresses for Bon Appetit's senior management. I type these addresses into the cc field. I also include the Dean of Student Life, and Dale from Student Support Services. I review the email one more time. Satisfied, I hit send.

Wait. How would I file a lawsuit? I don't know any disability rights lawyers. I can't even afford a lawyer. New questions begin kicking up doubt. How long do I wait for him to respond? If he agrees, how will I know if he really means it?

This is actually the perfect place to strike out into the unknown. Lewis & Clark College celebrates the history of America's pioneers—the college has a centrally located statue of Sacagawea, the Native American woman who served as an interpreter for the explorers Meriwether Lewis and William Clark. The college football team is called the Pioneers. The college newspaper is the *Pioneer Log*. The college shuttle is the Pioneer Express. The shuttle's destination? Pioneer Square.

The college's pioneer pride strengthens my commitment to my efforts. Everyone I've talked to at the college, from Student Support Services to the Assistant Dean of Student Life, has asked Bon Appetit to make the menus accessible. I don't know exactly how I'll convince Bon Appetit to comply, but I'm determined to try. Sending that email feels like as good a start as any. Besides, learning about the ADA will only benefit me in the long run. The next time I encounter someone unwilling to remove access barriers—and I will—I'll know what to do.

At lunch the next day, Gordon and I are sitting at a corner table in the cafeteria. The two walls behind us absorb some of the background noise.

"Have you heard from Claude?" Gordon asks.

"Nope. Not a word." I bite into a cheese and mushroom quesadilla.

"That doesn't surprise me." He takes a bite of his quesadilla. "My mom called this morning. They found a bear in their garage."

"What?" I gasp. "Did you say your mom found a bear in the garage?"

"Yeah, it managed to pull the garage door open and walk inside."

I look at him with alarm. "Is your family okay?"

"Yeah, everyone's fine. The bear didn't get into the main part of the house."

"Thank God! Wow, I could never live in Alaska. Remind me, what are you supposed to do when you encounter a bear?"

"The main thing is: don't run. Never, ever, run from a bear. Oh, here comes Claude."

A large man pulls out the chair next to mine. "How are you guys doing?"

My body tenses with appprehension, and I can barely speak. "Fine. And you?"

"Good. Listen, I'm really sorry about the menu situation. Let's start over. I've talked to everyone and we're going to do a better job going forward."

Memories of all our past conversations flash through my mind, leaving me with a heavy skepticism. "Will the emails come on time and consistently?"

"Yes. Everyone in the office understands this is important."

I take a deep breath. "Thank you—I appreciate that." Time will tell if he keeps his promise.

"Great." He stands up and puts something on the table. "I brought you guys chocolate chip cookies."

My hands stay in my lap. I give him a nod.

"If you need anything else, just let me know." He walks away.

Gordon leans over to me. "Someone must have really kicked his butt."

"Maybe, but how do we know if he really means it?" I pull one of the cookies toward me. "Do you think it's an olive branch or a hush cookie?"

"Haben!"

I laugh, releasing some of the tension. "I'm trying to figure out if I should eat it." The large, plastic-wrapped cookie feels soft and warm, like it recently came out of an oven. I turn it over in my hands, wondering what I should do. Unwrapping the cookie releases the mouthwatering smell of warm chocolate. "I'll give him another chance. See what happens."

A year later, the Bon feels different. Claude kept his promise, and the staff now provide accessible menus. Access to the menus reduces the stress of stepping into the cacophonous cafeteria. Eating vegetarian is much easier. Framing the access barrier as a civil rights issue rather than an act of charity helped shift the culture in the cafeteria.

The menu said station two has cheese tortellini, so I walk straight there. "Cheese tortellini," I tell the server when I reach the counter. The server places a plate on my tray. "Thank you."

The tables along the wall are quietest, so I head there. As I approach the tables, I slow down, squinting at each table to see if any are empty. I reach the last table, which is also occupied.

A young woman stops next to me. "Are you looking for your friend?"

I stare at her in confusion. "Yeah..."

The woman starts walking, and I follow her. She stops by the second table along the wall. "Here he is!"

When I walk up to the person at the table, I spot a long white cane next to him.

"Hi, Bill!"

"Hey, Haben." Bill is a first-year student from New Mexico who is also blind. People here talk loudly to him, so he keeps trying to explain that he's not me.

I thank the woman as she walks away. Then I settle into a chair. "So! I was just walking around looking for a table. This student comes up and goes, 'Are you looking for your friend?'"

"And she brought you to me?"

"Yes!"

"Because all blind people must be friends, right?"

"Apparently!" Laughing, I plunge a fork into the source of the tantalizing aroma of hot cheesy pasta. "Hey Bill, does the Bon email you menus?"

"Yes, actually—it's been really helpful."

"Just curious. You're hearing, so couldn't you hear someone reading the menu to you?"

"Sometimes. The cafeteria is really loud and it's hard to hear people, even for me, so the emails help a lot."

"Wow. I didn't realize it was hard for hearing people in here, too. I'm glad they're sending you the menus."

Bill's answer produces a stunning realization. My advocacy affects our entire community. The changes I worked for create greater access for me and for future blind students at Lewis & Clark. I remember wondering if my access to the menus was really worth all the time and energy needed to achieve that access. For a while I thought maybe I had to just tolerate the situation. Running away from a problem doesn't make it go away, though. Run from a bear and it chases you. That problem might have followed me through all four years of college if I hadn't stood my ground.

After talking to Bill, I start poking around online, looking up law schools all across the country. Just out of curiosity.

Chapter Nineteen

Alaska Gives Me the Cold, Harsh Truth

Juneau, Alaska. Summer 2008.

"We shouldn't have hired you." The manager's words send a bucket of glacier water dripping down my back.

I flew to Juneau, Alaska—right after my second year of college—thinking I had this cool job leading tours of the Capitol Building. The recruiters knew about my deafness, and we agreed I would receive questions and comments during the tours through my assistive technology. They knew about my racial status—I checked the box for African American on the application. There was just one thing they didn't know until I arrived at the Capitol. When I walked in for orientation this morning, the manager pulled me aside.

The manager's cramped office feels suffocating. We sit across from each other with our knees almost touching. My back straightens as I prepare to speak. "Are you telling me to leave because I'm blind?"

"No. It's because you're from California. These jobs are supposed to go to Alaskan residents."

My stomach drops. I sit there, speechless, until the shock shifts to injustice. "The paperwork showed that I'm from California. We even did the interview over the phone because I don't live here. You've known that for weeks. Why did you hire me if the position was only for Alaskans?"

"We made a mistake. I'm sorry."

Outside, a light rain drizzles over Juneau. The cold seeps through my coat, feeding the fear rising in the pit of my stomach. No one will hire me.

Gordon has a job working for a tour company. His sister works for another tour company. His brother supervises a summer youth program. Gordon's father leads wilderness and wildlife photography tours. A family friend also staying at the house works with at-risk youth. Laurie, Gordon's mom, teaches music. Everyone has a job except me.

Laurie rescues me from the Capitol Building, denouncing their dismissal the whole drive home. "You'll find a better job, Haben. Juneau has lots of summer jobs."

I nod, too dejected to speak.

When we arrive at the cozy house in the woods, I head straight to the computer. Craigslist has numerous job openings—Laurie was right. After the government, the tourism industry is the second largest employer in Juneau. Over a million tourists visit each summer for the city's spectacular scenery, abundance of wildlife, and majestic Mendenhall Glacier. Many employers turn to the Lower 48 to fill their summer openings. Of course, the ads don't mention Juneau's persistent precipitation.

Over the next weeks I send out dozens of applications, focusing on those that match my strengths in public speaking. Since helping to build a school in Mali, I've logged in numerous hours speaking to audiences big and small. My experience impressed the Capitol Building recruiters enough to choose me over Alaskans, at least until I walked in with a white cane. The applications lead to interviews, the interviews lead to rejections. Back on Craigslist, I broaden my search, responding to ads that seek people with strong reading, writing, or analytical skills. The pattern continues: submit an application, brave an interview, then face a rejection. I change my strategy, responding to nearly all the ads: shelving gift stores, baking cakes, folding laundry in hotels. Rejection. Rejection. Rejection.

Disability professionals warned me: work hard or you'll never find employment. Around seventy percent of blind people are unemployed. I studied hard in school, graduating high school as valedictorian. I spent a summer sharpening my independence skills at the Louisiana Center for the Blind. My college GPA is excellent. I even have volunteer work experience on my résumé. The seventy percent unemployment rate still managed to claim me, leaving me jobless in Jobville, Alaska.

When you do everything right and society stomps on you, over and over, it creates a piercing, gut-twisting pain. It causes you to question the conventional wisdom that a person who works hard will always overcome obstacles.

Gordon offers encouragement, but I don't want to hear it. He drummed up Alaska as the land of long summer days where the sun doesn't set until 10 p.m. He promised that I'd find a summer job here. Instead, I find employment discrimination.

Blindness is just the lack of sight, but people inflate the disability to an absurd degree. They assume incompetence, intellectual challenges, and an inability to contribute with alternative techniques. This is decades of cultural stories perpetuating the idea that people with disabilities are inferior to the nondisabled. Wherever I go, regardless of how hard I work, I keep encountering ableism.

Laurie bakes chocolate macaroons. The alluring aroma of warm chocolate pulls me away from the computer—just for a spell. While everyone else is at work, she invites me on a hike along the waterfalls of the steep Perseverance Trail. Feeling the sun on my face as I breathe in the smells of a mountain creek rushing through grass and trees helps me forget that I'm an unemployed failure—possibly forever.

Then Laurie recommends me to her friend Rachel, the manager of a local gym. Rachel reviews my résumé, interviews me, and hires me as a part-time front desk clerk. On our tour of the gym, Rachel teaches me how to use the machines, clean up the changing rooms, and manage the cash register. My white cane doesn't faze her at all. Whether I use sight or a nonvisual technique matters less than whether I get the job done.

One day a woman walks up to the front desk. "Hi, I'm trying to use a treadmill but it's not working."

"I'll take a look. Which one?" I follow her to a row of treadmills. She stops by the second machine. Setting my cane down, I step up to the machine and press the on button. Nothing. I try the other buttons on the panel. Nothing. Using both hands, I search the machine from top to bottom. Along the base I find a switch. When I flick it, the treadmill whirs to life.

"Oh my god, thank you! That was amazing! I didn't even see that switch," she says.

My lips turn up in a playful grin. "I didn't see it, either."

We laugh, a cathartic, soul-healing laugh.

Sometimes tactile techniques beat visual techniques. Someday the world will learn that people with disabilities are talented, too.

Chapter Twenty

The Little Dog That Makes Earthquakes

Morristown, New Jersey. Summer 2009.

"You need to trust Maxine," my instructor says. George and I are standing on a sidewalk in downtown Morristown, New Jersey. Instead of battling employment discrimination this summer, I've decided to train with a guide dog. "Feel what she's doing through the harness."

I nod. Maxine is a highly trained Seeing Eye dog. She spent the first two years of her life with The Seeing Eye, the oldest guide dog school in the United States. Over the last few months, George has provided Maxine with extensive training to prepare her for a life of guiding.

"If she makes a mistake, correct her by saying 'no,' or, if it's something serious, say 'pfui' in a mean voice." *Pfui*, pronounced "foo-EE," is a German exclamation of deep displeasure. "It's more important to praise her, though, so give her lots of praise and encouragement. She has to want to guide you."

I drop down to Maxine's level and begin petting her. "You're a good girl, Maxine."

For a German shepherd, she's actually quite small: at fifty pounds, she's almost half the size of the other shepherds, but her size is perfect for me. Maxine has smooth black and tan fur that turns super soft along her adorable ears. Her cute long nose points, probes, and pushes my hand to request more petting. She's completely charmed me after only one day together.

"Have her take you around the block. Start by going to this next corner."

"Okay." I stand up and get into position. My left hand holds a leash and harness designed by The Seeing Eye. Soft leather straps wrap around the dog's back, chest, and front. An adjustable buckle helps ensure the fit is comfortable. The straps connect to a light handle that rests across the dog's back. Holding the handle with my left hand, I gesture forward with my right. "Maxine, forward."

She charges ahead, yanking my arm. I jog to keep up, until I remember that a little tension in the connection helps a leader guide a follower on the dance floor. Feeling for tension in the harness handle, I switch to a brisk walk. Centering myself, I concentrate on making long quick strides to match her four fast feet. My left foot slams into a large crack in the sidewalk. Stumbling, I hop up and keep walking. Maxine continues pulling forward. Inside my shoes, I curl my toes up to minimize tripping. Maxine leads me through more uneven sidewalk, and this time I maintain my balance. Then she stops where the sidewalk ends.

"Good girl!" I scratch her ears.

"How was that?" George asks.

"Awesome!"

"Was she going too fast?"

"No way. That was fun."

"Okay. If she goes too fast you can tell her to slow down."

"Mhm."

"I want you to tell her to turn left and walk to the end of this block."

"Maxine, left." She turns left. "Maxine, forward."

She pads along, and my long strides help me keep up. I breathe deeply, centering myself. My feet glide over uneven terrain. Then Maxine stops at the next corner.

"Good girl! What a good girl, Maxine!" I drop to her level and massage her neck.

"That was great," George says. "Keep going."

I stand up. "Maxine, left." We reposition ourselves and I give her the forward command again.

My left hand feels a strong tug, and I immediately move with it. My legs take long quick strides as all my attention zooms in on the leather harness connected to Maxine. Little tremors climb up the harness to the handle every time she steps forward. Left, right, left, right. I marvel at how much tactile information travels through the harness handle.

My foot smashes into an object. I'm falling. My hands and feet jerk out, breaking the fall at the last second. My legs tremble as I stand back up.

George arrives. "Say *pfui*."

My voice feels trapped in my throat. I take a deep breath and utter a fierce "*Pfui!*"

Maxine steps back, upset. I'm upset, too. She walked me right into some potted plants.

"Are you hurt?" George asks.

I consider the question for a moment. "No."

"Okay. Turn to the right and have her go forward, back to the sidewalk, then continue around the block."

Hesitating, I look down at the little dog. She tripped me! A Seeing Eye dog tripped me!

I adjust the leash and harness to the proper position. "Maxine, forward." She takes two steps, then stops. I put more authority in my voice. "Forward." She starts walking again. "Maxine, left." Several steps later she turns left. Back on the sidewalk she picks up speed. My toes reach for the sky, anticipating another fall. When we reach the end of the block, we stop.

"Praise her," George says.

I give him an incredulous look. "She tripped me."

"That was earlier. You corrected her when she made a mistake. When she does something right, she needs to be praised. She just guided you to this corner, and you should praise her."

"Okay." I lean down and scratch Maxine's ears. "Good girl! Good girl, Maxine!" I straighten up. "Why did she trip me? I thought you trained her."

"It takes time for a dog and human to develop a working relationship. If it worked from day one then we wouldn't need a three-and-a-half-week training program. You're going to have to be patient. These things take time."

I frown skeptically, still upset.

"Let's go back inside." George leads the way to the training center. It's a large room with couches and armchairs where students and instructors congregate.

I find a spot on the couch and sit down. "Maxine, sit." She ignores me until I gently push her butt down. "Good girl!"

"Hey, Haben!" A woman calls to me from the other end of the couch. "How was your walk?" Keianna is from Chicago. She's here to train with her third guide dog and doesn't mind answering my rookie questions.

I scoot over to sit next to her. "Maxine tried to kill me."

"What! What happened?"

I describe the incident to her, and Keianna laughs. "Honey, that happens to everyone. The dogs are going to mess up during training. You have to trust your dog."

"I trusted her, and she tripped me!"

"Aww, she didn't mean it."

I mutter darkly, "Uh huh, sure."

Keianna chuckles. "Trust me, it gets better. It's like dating. The first date is a little awkward, but over time the relationship grows stronger."

I look down at the dog stretched out on the floor by my feet. "I'm sure you're right." I get up, and Maxine leaps to her feet. I smile. "I'm going to go find something to read." Reaching down, I grasp Maxine's harness. "Maxine, forward." We walk across the room, Maxine in the lead. She stops. Glancing down, I observe her sitting with her head bent down and her tail straight out. Puzzled, I just stare. Then it hits me: she's peeing! She's peeing indoors! Shock freezes my limbs like an arctic wind. Then George's advice cracks through the ice. I lean down close to her ear. *"Pfui!"* She keeps peeing. I try my meanest voice. *"Pfui!"*

"Good job correcting her." Peggy, another instructor, steps over to us. "It's okay, I'll clean this up."

I hesitate. Shouldn't I be the one to clean up after my dog? The instructor did offer, though. "Thanks." I wave for Maxine to keep moving. "Forward." I carry a braille magazine back to the couch and grumble, "Maxine just peed in here."

"Bob's dog just peed in here, too. They act up sometimes during training," Keianna explains.

I shake my head. "I thought they were trained."

"They are trained. I told you, relationships take time."

I open the magazine on my lap. "As far as first dates go, this one's pissy."

By nine in the evening I'm ready to sleep. The Seeing Eye gives every student their own dorm room. I tie Maxine by her dog bed and climb into my human bed beside her. She sits up next to my bed. "You're a good girl, Maxine." I pet her. When I stop, she pokes me with her nose. "Sweetie, you need to sleep." I pull the comforter over my head. Her long nose pokes my arm through the comforter. I ignore it. Then her two front legs claw me. "Ow! Down!" She continues standing, her head on my bed. I jump out of bed and kneel next to hers. "Sit." She obeys. "Good girl! Good, Maxine!" As I scratch her ears, she leans into my hands. I massage her neck, her shoulders, her back. "Down." She lies down on her bed, and I continue petting her. "Good girl, Maxine. Brava, Maxine. Goodnight, Maxine." I stand up, and she leaps to her feet. "That's enough." I walk around the bed and get in on the opposite side.

Exhausted, I fall asleep. Sleep takes me to a world where imagination reigns. The typical five senses become irrelevant—my sight and hearing mirror my waking world. I'm Deafblind, but information reaches me without the usual struggle. I effortlessly identify people, receive messages, and experience phenomena. The knowledge just emerges from within, as if it were there all along. I dream about being home in California. My sister and I sit in our living room, sipping Saba's cinnamon tea. Then our house starts shaking. Earthquake!

I bolt up in bed. My heart pounds in my chest. That earthquake felt real. Are there earthquakes in New Jersey?

Just then, the bed starts shaking.

Earthquake!

The tremors feel stronger on my right side. I push off the comforter and crawl to the right. Then I stop. Maxine's front half is on the bed. Confused, I stay just outside her reach, waiting. She watches me, too. Then she scratches the mattress with lightning speed, like a dog digging a hole. The whole bed shakes.

"You're a little earthquake, Maxine." Laughing, I start petting her. She leans her head into my hand. Climbing out of bed, I kneel beside her. She jumps off the bed and nudges me with her nose. "The Seeing Eye says no dogs on the bed. Sorry." As I run my hands over her to check if anything is wrong, she continues to poke and paw me. "You're fine, baby girl. Down." She drops down and rolls over. I rub her belly. "Good girl, Maxine. Goodnight, Maxine." When I stand up, she stands up, too. I crawl back into bed and pull the comforter over me. The bed begins to shake. I tune it out and slip back to sleep.

Over the next week, Maxine and I go through many hours of training. George watches as we navigate sidewalks, cross streets, and maneuver through stores. When Maxine walks me into something, I correct her. When she does something well, I praise her. She receives a lot of praise, especially during the traffic checks. While Maxine and I cross streets, she guides us out of the way as instructors pretend to run us down with their cars.

When I'm not training with Maxine, I'm studying for the Law School Admission Test (LSAT). I brought practice braille tests, and I keep a digital copy of the practice materials on my laptop, which I access using screenreader software.

I'm sitting at my desk typing a response to an essay prompt when Maxine paws my leg. I drop my hands from the keyboard and start petting her. "Down." I continue petting her as she lies down. "Good girl! Now rest."

My hands back on the keyboard, I begin typing. The first time I tried responding to a practice LSAT prompt, my brain froze. The correct answer felt a million miles away. I'm doing this, I told myself. Right or wrong, I needed to start. So I made myself type that first sentence. Feedback from the first essay I wrote has helped make each new one easier to write. I don't even have to think to know what I want to write for this one. My fingers fly over the keyboard as I type out another sentence.

Maxine paws my leg. I keep typing. She paws my leg again. My hands stay on the keyboard. Maxine shoves her long nose against my left wrist, launching my hand into the air.

I laugh. "You're so persistent!" She leans into my hands as I pet her. "I need to study or I'll never get into law school. Down. Good girl! Rest."

Sitting back up in my chair, I continue typing. A few seconds later, Maxine pushes my arm off the keyboard with her nose. Regaining control of my left arm, I put it back down on the keyboard. The muscles clench, preparing for another assault. The nose pushes my arm again, but this time my arm stays put. She shoves harder, lifting my arm two inches off the keys.

"No," I gently admonish. "Boundaries. I need you to respect my work time. We'll play later." With that, I turn back to my computer.

She tries the nose launch two more times. After not getting a response, she stretches out on the floor. I continue studying.

The next interruption comes through the PA system. Lunchtime!

Maxine and I step out into the hall. My left hand has her leash and harness. "Forward!" She starts walking down the hall, past other dorm rooms. I encourage her to go faster, "Hup up." She launches herself forward, doubling her speed. "Good girl!" We dash down the hall, curve left through a little lobby, and skid to a stop. "Good girl!" Reaching with one foot, I tap the top of the staircase. "Forward." We bound down the stairs together. "Good girl! Forward." She starts walking down the hall. "Hup up," I urge. Down the hall we fly, Maxine and I. We whiz past another student. "Good girl! Go, Maxine!"

"Haben!"

I stop, and Maxine stops, too.

George walks over. "You need to slow down."

"Why?"

"Maxine has less time to think when she's going that fast. Besides, we have other students here. Two blind people walking that fast, *kaboom!*"

I grin. "Okay, we'll slow down in busy areas." I wave my hand toward the dining room. "Maxine, forward."

She walks a few feet, and then stops. Just like she did the other day, Maxine drops to a sitting position with her head bent forward and her tail straight out.

I stomp my foot. She keeps peeing. I channel my fury into one word, "*Pfui!*" Maxine stands up. I immediately walk us back to George. "She just peed! Last week she peed in the downtown training center. Why is she doing this? She's supposed to be house-trained."

"Have you taken her outside this morning?"

"Yes. Twice."

"She didn't do this when I was training her."

I give him an incredulous look. "What does that mean?"

"I'm pretty sure she's housebroken. Just give her time. You two are doing really well together. Don't worry—I'll clean this up. You guys go on to lunch."

Maxine and I enter the dining room. Students sit around long tables, and dogs lie underneath. I direct Maxine to the end of a table near a wall where it's a little quieter. A woman with shoulder length black hair has the end seat; a black Lab lies at her feet.

"Hello." I slide into the seat next to her.

"Hey, Haben!"

"Stacy, right?" Stacy is an experienced guide dog handler from Wisconsin.

"Yeah." She reaches under the table to check on her dog, London.

Maxine's back nestles against my shoes. I keep my feet still so she can nap. "How was your morning?"

"It was terrible."

My eyes widen. "What went wrong?"

"Oh...everything."

"Everything?" My pitch rises as I draw out the word.

"Yeah." She laughs. "But it was all my fault. I made a mistake."

Maxine stands up, turns around, and lies back down. She drapes a paw over my right shoe. "So what happened?" I ask Stacy.

"I got lost in a parking lot."

"Oh no!"

"I spent like ten minutes trying to get out." Amusement and frustration mingle in her voice. "I figured it out, though, eventually."

"That's good." I ponder her story for a minute. "How did you get into the parking lot in the first place?"

She answers in a quiet, sheepish voice, "That was London."

"These dogs!" I laugh. "Mine has been getting into trouble, too. She peed in the hallway today, and last week she peed in the training center downtown. She wakes me up in the middle of the night, so I never get a full night's sleep. It's like I'm parenting a newborn."

"But we love them regardless, don't we? Because they give us freedom and independence."

Reaching for a glass of water on the table, I decide to keep my thoughts on that remark to myself.

My freedom and independence come from me. My confidence comes from within. Choosing to partner with a guide dog is a choice. It's not better or worse than a cane, just different. A cane would catch a row of plants, preventing me from tripping over them. A cane would let me sleep instead of interrupting my dreams with earthquakes. A cane doesn't pee. The power of the simple device has a breathtaking elegance. Maybe I should stick with using a cane.

But then, walking with a dog feels amazing. Maxine moves smoothly through space, gliding around obstacles with ease. A cane would need to first make contact with an obstacle before I could walk around it. Also, holding the harness for a long time doesn't exhaust my arm the way holding a cane does. With additional eyes and ears, the dog offers more environmental feedback, more safety while crossing streets, more security navigating the world.

I would rather walk with a guide dog than a cane, but peeing indoors is a dealbreaker. My future involves classrooms and courtrooms, law school and law firms. Professionalism necessitates navigating those spaces without dog urine. Maxine is a sweet dog, but if she keeps this up I'm going to have to resume using a cane.

After a long day of training, Maxine and I visit the student lounge before heading to bed. "Hello?" The room seems empty. Sitting down on the couch, I take out my iPhone. Apple just created VoiceOver, a screenreader that converts graphical data on the screen to synthesized speech. It's the first speech synthesizer that I can actually hear—the high-frequency voice falls within my limited range of hearing, and earbuds allow me to bring the sound directly to my ears. The revolutionary VoiceOver has created access to the iPhone and an array of powerful tools now available on the go—GPS, email, books, and the internet. I'm still blown away by the fact that I can actually text people.

Maxine jumps up. I look up and notice several people entering the room. They talk among themselves. I can't hear the conversation, so I go back to my phone.

"What are you doing?" a voice asks.

I study the person sitting next to me: a guy about my height, with a black Lab. I smile. "Hi, Country Kid."

A woman on the other side of the couch cheers. Keianna! She came up with the nickname after Peter regaled her with stories from rural Texas.

"Are you going to answer my question?" Peter asks.

"I'm texting."

"Who?" he demands to know.

"Gordon. He's from Alaska."

"Whoa. Does he have an accent like Sarah Palin?"

"I don't know. I'll ask him." Imagining Gordon's reaction makes me laugh.

The man on my right calls out, "Someone's dog is licking my feet." Sebastian is a religious leader in Florida and wears black robes. An instructor said they partnered Sebastian with a black Lab to match his cassock.

Inspecting Maxine's nose, I find it by Sebastian's feet. "Baby girl, that's not professional. Come on, move just a little bit. Good, Maxine! Good girl!" She stretches out on the floor facing a different direction.

"The way you talk to her is so sweet," Sebastian says.

"That's because I'm not speaking German."

He chuckles. *"Como te llamas?"* He asks for my name.

I'm surprised. We've all been in this program for three weeks now. *"Me llamo* Haben."

"Heaven? *Como cielo?"*

My mind takes a moment to translate his words through my limited high school Spanish. When I get it, I try to suppress my mirth. "No, not *como cielo.* My name is Haben. Though I am heavenly."

The room bursts into laughter. The sound makes my heart dance. Getting people to laugh diffuses any disability-related awkwardness. Humor draws people in, paving the way for meaningful connections. At some point in my childhood I discovered the goodwill sparked by bringing laughter into people's lives, and I've been developing my sense of humor ever since.

Sebastian switches to English. "Haben, Peter is calling you."

"Oh." I turn around on the couch to face Peter. "Did you say something?"

"Yeah. I was wondering, could you get me a drink?"

"I could. Or maybe I should let you practice being independent."

"Nooo!" he wails. "That wouldn't be kind at all!"

"Just this once." Standing up, I gesture to Maxine. "Maxine, forward. Good girl!" Halfway across the room, she stops to pee. My blood boils. *"Pfui! Pfui!"* Taking deep breaths, I try to calm down. "Keianna, Maxine just peed!"

"It's okay. She's still learning. Babies mess up sometimes."

I march off to a shelf with cleaning supplies. Grabbing paper towels and a cleaner, I return to the carpet. I tear off a few sheets of paper towel, fold them over, and drag them over the carpet searching for the wet spot. Maxine nudges my arm. "Sit. Rest." I hesitate, then mumble, "Good girl."

After cleaning up and washing my hands, I announce to the room, "I'm going to bed."

"Are you upset?" Keianna asks.

"Yes." Maxine follows as I walk over to Keianna. "We've been here three weeks and she's still having accidents."

"It gets better over time. Trust me. They act up during training, but after training everything gets better. Just don't go to bed mad at your baby."

Sighing, I stand up. "Maybe she's not cut out to be a guide dog." The words squeeze my heart, foreshadowing the pain of a breakup. I walk to my room with a lump in my throat.

The following day, I tell George we need to talk. He takes a seat across from me in the student room.

"Maxine has been having a lot of accidents," I tell him. "They happen so often I don't even think they can be called 'accidents.' I don't think she's qualified to graduate. I can't take a dog that's not housebroken."

"Do you like your dog?" he asks.

I glance down at the dog sitting between us. Maxine points her ears, taking in every word. "I like her a lot. She's smart, she's sweet. She's a really cute dog. But that's not the point."

"And how's her guiding?" George continues, seeming to miss my concerns.

My temples throb with a headache. "I'm not complaining about her guiding. She's doing great. Every day she guides better and better. But she's still peeing inside! That's the issue."

"Maxine is an amazing dog. One of the best I've ever worked with. She didn't have accidents when I worked with her. Are you giving her opportunities to use the bathroom outside?"

Too frustrated to speak, I nod my head yes.

"And does she do anything when you take her outside?"

I nod again.

"Then you're doing just fine. Continue giving her opportunities to go outside."

"You don't understand. It's been *three weeks* and she's still having accidents. We're almost at the end of the program. I can't take a dog that pees inside."

"You don't have to take her. You can leave her here. It's your choice. But if I were you, I would take her. She's one of the best dogs I've ever seen. Really smart, really loves to please. You two have bonded well. She really likes you."

My eyes water. I struggle to hold back the tears. "I like her, too, but peeing inside is not acceptable. I plan to go to law school and become a lawyer. Traveling with a dog that has frequent accidents is unprofessional. Do you understand that it's not okay?"

"Of course. I agree with you. But she is house-trained. German shepherds are particularly sensitive and struggle with change. She's going through an adjustment process. It just takes time."

"When will she stop having accidents?"

"I can't give you an exact date. You can leave her here if you want. No one will force you to take her, but she's a wonderful dog. Give her more time."

I begin petting Maxine as my mind grapples with the decision. She is a lovely dog. I adore her. I didn't come here for a cute dog, though—I came here for a service animal, and a service animal that has accidents every other day is not acceptable.

What should I do?

I have a few weeks before fall college classes start. If she's still not house-trained by September, then I'll send her back to The Seeing Eye. I swallow, trying to clear the lump in my throat. "Okay, I'll give her more time."

"Excellent. Good choice. Anything else we need to discuss?"

I shake my head, still petting Maxine.

George stands up and heads to the door. "You two are doing great. Keep it up." He steps out and closes the door.

As I run my hands through Maxine's soft fur, I give her the update. "Pumpkin, you're on probation."

Maxine has memorized the routes to all of my college classes, and her favorite path is the one we take to go home. Once I give her the signal, her four legs start working double-time, just short of a run. Her excitement travels up the harness, through my arm, and up to my mirroring smile. Maxine moves with an elegance that earns respect from everyone around us. My classmates and professors call her perfect. I pet her, praise her, and sometimes correct her. They're right, though. She's perfect.

Maxine hasn't had an accident since leaving The Seeing Eye three months ago. Not a single one. Not even during our eight-hour journey back to Oregon. Looking at her now is like looking at an adult and trying to remember the person as a two-year-old going through potty training.

During training she didn't care about me enough to keep me safe or keep the carpets clean. Love takes time. Love forms through the expression of genuine appreciation, the creation of clear boundaries, the practice of forgiveness, and mutual respect. Over time, these experiences weave together, forming a strong bond between two beings. Time and experience have fostered a trust that draws us together, building a shared understanding that continues to grow.

There's another big change: Maxine stopped making earthquakes. Nowadays, I let her sleep on my bed. She promised not to tell The Seeing Eye.

Chapter Twenty-One

Love Is Following Me up an Iceberg

Juneau, Alaska. Winter 2010.

Despite heavy gloves, my fingers feel numb as I scramble up the iceberg on my hands and feet. This iceberg stands just a half mile away from the Mendenhall Glacier.

Located in Juneau, Alaska, the Mendenhall Glacier is one of the most spectacular places on planet Earth. Every so often, the glacier drops icebergs into the large lake in front of it. Gordon, his friend Sam, and I were walking across the frozen lake toward the glacier when we discovered the most incredible iceberg. It's The Iceberg of icebergs. It rose right out of a dream: a round hill on one side, and on the other...a perfect ice slide!

Of course we want to climb it and slide down. Sam went first a few minutes ago; now Gordon and I are climbing the steep hill. My arms feel shaky. I could slip, or the great glacier could calve, or the lake could crack, or this iceberg could fall apart. I quiet my fears, reminding myself that every adventure has a risk. Besides, Sam and Gordon grew up playing on this lake. When in Alaska, do as the Alaskans do.

"No!" Behind me, Maxine has started walking up the iceberg. I pack authority into my voice, "No!" Maxine keeps climbing. Fear pulses through my veins. *"Pfui!"* She reaches me seven feet up the icy hill. "You weren't supposed to follow me up here! Maxeeny, this isn't safe. You need to get down."

I call up the iceberg to Gordon. "Hang on! I'm going to take Maxine down. I'll be right back."

Climbing backward, I carefully make my way down. "Maxeeny, come!" She turns toward me. "Good girl! Come!" My feet reach a smooth surface. The lake. I stand up. "Maxeeny, you can do it. Come." She leaps off the iceberg and lands by my feet. "Good girl! Don't ever do that again."

I walk over to Sam. He lives here in Juneau and has been Gordon's close friend since grade school. "Would you hold Maxine for me?" I hand her leash to Sam.

"Sure, no problem."

"Thanks, Sam. Bye, Maxine! Be good." I pet her back, and it feels strange having a glove between us. It's winter break of my senior year. I've been in Alaska for a few days now, but I'm still not used to having my hands covered.

I cautiously walk back up the hill of ice. The iceberg becomes steep about five feet up, whereupon I lower myself to my hands and feet. My gloves sweep the ice before sinking the weight of my body into my hands. My feet, encased in thick wool socks and winter boots, test a step before placing my weight down. The surface has smooth areas, bumpy areas where solid chunks of ice protrude out of the hill, and areas with a layer of loose, tiny pieces of ice and snow.

Reaching above me brings something new into focus. A new protrusion to grip. A new hole in the ice to perch a foot. My feet slip often as I survey the slope through my boots until I land on a solid foothold.

Every few steps I squint and search for Gordon's red-and-black parka. Its contrast against the ice enhances his visibility as he waits for me to catch up. Sam powered through this slippery slope three times faster than me. Gordon can climb fast, too, but he's not here to race. He wants to introduce me to this glorious winter wonderland.

As I climb, the red-and-black parka looms closer and closer. The hill levels, and I realize I've reached the top. My arms balance my weight as I carefully turn and sit next to Gordon. Sitting on the biting cold surface is unpleasant, but my arms and legs sigh with relief. I survey the world I've just conquered, a dazzling bluish white world of ice. The fact that this is all water fills me with awe. I've been walking on water, climbing water, sitting on water...

Gordon's voice startles me. "Well, well, well, if it isn't a Californian! Have you come to steal our ice?"

"If you cooperate, we'll let you keep half of the glacier." Gazing out on the world from my glacial throne, I spot a dark blob in the distance that must be Sam and Maxine. "How high up are we?"

"About twenty feet. By the way, Maxine is crying."

Guilt squeezes my heart. "It's okay, Maxine! Don't worry! I'll come back!" Poor Maxine. If I'd known we were going climbing today I would have left her at home. Maxine hates being separated from me—when something comes between us, she makes the most pitiful sounds. When I go skiing, she cries. When I go ice-skating, she cries. When I take a shower, she cries. Maxine hates having anything between us, even a bathroom door.

"She's watching you with her ears pointed. If Sam weren't holding her leash she'd probably be up here with us."

I shudder. She could slip. She could fall. "Thanks for watching her, Sam!"

Sam shouts something.

Gordon relays the message. "He's saying he sees huge cracks in the ice where I'm sitting. He's lying."

My mind pictures the ice shattering, dropping us into an abyss. "Let's move. Where's the slide?"

Gordon gets on his hands and knees, crawling a few feet to the right. "Come over here, but stay to my right."

My arms tremble as I crawl along the ice wall beside Gordon.

He guides my hand four feet to the left. "This is the edge. It's about a twenty-foot drop." He moves my hand to the right. "On this side there's a wall. Stay in the middle and you'll be fine."

Sam starts shouting.

"He's cheering," Gordon explains.

I smile. So many people would scold me with a persistent chorus of "You can't! You shouldn't! You won't!" But Sam and Gordon are the opposite: not only do they share their Alaskan playground, they cheer me on, too. Even Maxine doesn't hold me back; she just wants to be by my side.

"Are you ready?" Gordon asks.

"No." I blush, embarrassed. "Is there anything else I should know? Anything else you should describe?"

"Umm, no, not really. Just stay away from the edge on the left and you'll be fine."

I move an inch forward, then stop. My stomach is in knots. My mind keeps conjuring up calamities: what if I lose control on the ice? What if the slide has a bend and I miss it because I can't see it? Every cell in my body is telling me not to slide into the unknown. "Any more descriptions?" My voice cracks, and I try to steady it. "Anything else I should know?"

"Maxine still has her eyes on you. She wants her mommy."

Oh no, she's going to watch her mommy fall off an ice cliff. I scoot back from the slide. "Can you go first? Then I can sort of follow you."

"Sure." He sits down in front of me, and then pushes off. Slowly at first, then faster, the red-and-black parka zips out of sight.

I stretch my hand to the left and feel the edge. Danger on the left, I remind myself. Scooting forward, I feel for the wall on my right. My legs stretch out in front of me, poised to glide down an iceberg slide.

A deep shiver travels down my spine. Relax, I tell myself. Stop being scared.

The cliff, the slide, and the entire lake fuse into a shimmery white. I can't see the edge of the slide. Facing the unknown usually doesn't faze me. My inability to see the path ahead when I'm walking down a street with Maxine doesn't scare me. Not in the slightest. I know that if I tripped or fell on the sidewalk, I'd just hop back up. Here, the slippery ice impairs my movement, creating a kind of mobility disability on top of my Deafblindness. If I slip, it's a twenty-foot drop.

Shouting reaches me from below.

Maybe they're cheering again. I smile.

More shouting.

What if they're trying to warn me? What if the iceberg cracked? Heart pounding, I peer over the edge. Nothing. I listen with all my might. Nothing.

My hands push off the ice, launching me forward. I go speeding, slipping, sliding. My body leans to the right as my hand presses against the wall, a wall once part of the grand glacier. My left hand, spread out flat along the slide, helps steer me away from the left edge. The ice levels, and I come to a stop.

Maxine runs over with Sam right behind her.

"Maxeeny! See, I told you not to worry." I scratch her ears.

Sam steps closer. "Didn't you hear us yelling for you to stop?"

"I couldn't hear you." Panic squeezes my lungs as I wait for his dire news.

"We were telling you to wait until Gordon started filming."

My breath comes out in an extended, "Oh," traveling from apprehension to relief. They just want to get a video. A video of this incredible ice slide. "That's a great idea. Then I could show this place to my parents." My gaze turns to the iceberg. Once it looked tall and terrifying, an icy fortress in a frozen lake. Now I know a path up and over it. "I could slide down again so you can film it."

"It's getting dark," Gordon says. "How important is the video?"

Maxine nudges my hand with her nose. I move my hand over her head and start massaging her neck as she leans against me. The fact that she followed me up an iceberg both warms my heart and scares me. She'll probably try to follow me again, but she's too precious to make the climb.

My world shifts with a new realization: this is how my parents would feel if they saw me climbing icebergs. This is how they felt when I told them I wanted to travel to Mali. They wanted to stop me, even though they themselves had traveled through Africa. Now here I am, worrying about Maxine's safety with minimal concern for my own. Through Maxine, I'm starting to understand parental love and the paradox of taking personal risks while holding loved ones to a higher standard.

"Yeah, let's head back. We can do pictures another day." I turn to Maxine, my voice becoming excited. "I'm ready to go! Are you ready to go?"

Maxine hops up, twirls, and wags her tail. She won't have to endure any more separation from me—not until the next time I visit a bathroom.

Chapter Twenty-Two

The First Deafblind Student at Harvard Law School

Cambridge, Massachusetts. Fall 2010.

"Can you hear me?"

The loud voice coming through my earbuds sounds scratchy. The earbuds connect to an FM receiver, part of an assistive listening device. The receiver picks up sounds coming through the FM microphone. Harvard Law School hired American Sign Language interpreters with voice transliteration skills to provide access to audio and visual information in my classes. Celia Michau and Erin Foley sit in the back of the classroom whispering into a microphone covered by a small stenographer's mask. The microphone has a wireless connection with the receiver, so I can sit anywhere in the classroom. I prefer to sit in the back, though, just in case I need to communicate with the interpreters.

"[Mumble, mumble, static crackle.] How about now?" the voice asks.

I shrug, then shake my head no.

"Is this better?" Hissing static muffles the voice.

I shake my head again.

"Well, you're responding, so you can kind of hear us, right?"

Somewhere in front of me, the professor lectures us on contracts. Around him, seventy students sit in rows of desks facing forward. Using my voice would disrupt the class.

Turning to the back of the room, I lift my hands, then pause. To communicate through signs, I need to distill my ideas into my limited sign language vocabulary, or otherwise spell out all the words. I sign, "C-O-M-P-L-I-C-A-T-E-D."

"It's complicated? So you can hear us but it's hard to hear us?"

I sign, "Right."

"Okay. What can we do to help?"

"I don't know," I sign.

"The professor just looked at us. I think he was wondering if you raised your hand."

My face grows hot. I make a mental note to keep my signing as low as possible.

"Do you want us to continue with class?"

Nodding, I turn my chair to face the front.

"Okay, back to class. The defendant's [mumble mumble]."

The lecture continues, and I strain to catch the words. The sounds twist and turn in my ear. Every way I listen, the words are gobbledygook. It's not the volume—it's turned to a high setting. It's not comprehension, either; I've done the reading. It's my hearing. My ever-decreasing, diminishing, disappointing hearing.

I'm twenty-two years old, and every year my hearing and

vision have dimmed. The changes are too gradual to notice, until all of the sudden my old coping strategies no longer work. Since I wore sleepshades during blindness training, adjusting to my ongoing vision loss has been straightforward—I already have all the blindness skills. Adjusting to hearing loss feels more challenging. My low-frequency hearing has vanished. My limited high-frequency hearing has shrunk to a tiny sliver on my audiogram. The inaccessibility of the hearing world constantly threatens to isolate me.

My mind has developed a blueprint for English speech sounds. The blueprint sometimes converts the high-frequency sounds I manage to hear into an English word. The words I catch suggest sentences. The sentences suggest ideas. Lessons from the reading fill in the blanks. Reading got me through middle school, high school, and college; reading caught the ideas that slipped past my plummeting hearing. After class, a student will email class notes to the disability office; the office will then forward those notes to me. If I manage to survive law school, it's going to be because of reading.

The voice in my ear says, "This is Celia. Maxine has four paws in the air. So many questions!"

My shoulders shake. My fingers spell, "H-A H-A." Reaching down for Maxine, I discover her stretched out with all four paws in the air. I give her a belly rub.

"Okay, the professor is writing on the board. *Webb v. McGowin.* When we return from our break I want us to [mumble mumble]."

The room erupts in noise. The student next to me stands up and walks to the door.

Spinning around in my seat, I turn to Celia and Erin. "I can always tell when you're talking, but sometimes it's too muffled to understand the words. Sometimes there are static sounds. Other times I just can't hear the words and I don't know why."

Garbled speech comes through the earbuds.

"Sorry." I blush. "Now it's too loud in here."

Celia kneels in front of me. She slips her right hand under my left hand and starts signing.

"Sorry, I don't know those signs." My blush deepens. Interpreters spend years studying American Sign Language so they can easily communicate with Deaf people. My lack of fluency makes me feel like a difficult Deaf person—a person with communication challenges that even the experts can't solve.

Celia points to the door and fingerspells, "L-E-T-S T-A-L-K O-U-T-S-I-D-E."

"Okay." Carrying the FM receiver, I stand up and walk to the door. The three of us huddle in the quiet hall.

"Can you hear me now?" Erin asks.

I smile. "Yes. It's easier to hear you when you're not whispering."

"I bet. We've been trying to keep our voices down so that we don't distract the other students."

"I know. I don't want you to distract the other students, either."

Erin passes the microphone. "This is Celia. Do you have any idea what we could do to make it easier for you to hear us in the classroom?"

"I'm not sure. I hear you best when you speak loudly, clearly, and there is no background noise. I think the microphone is picking up the professor's voice. Maybe your voice is echoing in the stenographer mask. Plus, you have to whisper."

"That's a lot of variables. It's also possible that the radio frequency the FM system is using is experiencing interference with something in the room."

I nod. "Maybe."

"Gosh, I don't know, Haben. I'll keep thinking. Erin has something to say."

Erin takes the mic. "Before we go back in, I just wanted to let you know that this guy two rows in front of us has been texting under the table. He's trying to be subtle. It's hilarious. Every few minutes he looks down at his phone with this gleeful smile."

"Who?" While I've been making a supreme effort to hear, other students have been sprinkling mini visual breaks throughout class. Maybe I should find a way to reduce classroom stress, too.

"I don't know his name. I'll let you know if I figure it out."

The mic changes hands. "This is Celia. Just let us know if there is anything specific you're curious about. Obviously we're going to focus on the lecture, but if there are specific visual descriptions you want us to give you, just let us know."

"I'm interested in social descriptions—the little details that create personality, the little quirks that make people human."

"Yeah, that makes sense. We'll try to do that. Shall we go back in?"

We walk back into the classroom and take our seats.

Loud conversations ricochet around the room. The exact words stay beyond my reach. Several students stand beside the table in the next row. The group bursts into laughter. I can hear the merriment, can see the merriment, and still feel that old glass wall keeping me on the outside looking in.

I turn on my braille computer and begin reading case notes.

The sound of chattering students continues to bombard my ears. There's laughter. More conversation. Laughter again. My inner ear hears four devastating little words: you're being left out.

I start petting Maxine.

The buzzing persists, pounding my eardrums. *You're being left out.* Massaging Maxine's neck, I struggle to tune out the noise.

A hand touches my arm. I turn. Celia, kneeling in front of me, slips her right hand under my left. I reach out with my right hand and place it on top of her left. She starts signing.

"Slow down." My fingers probe her hand shapes as I drag sign language lessons out of the deep recesses of my memory. "L-I-Q-I-N Liqin I-S is...Sorry, I don't know that sign. A-S-K-I-N-G asking...I'm sorry, I don't know that one." My face burns from embarrassment. "W-H-A-T Oh, right! I did know that sign. Sorry, go on. What...is your dog's name, question mark."

I look around. Someone is standing to the right of Celia. Liqin. I address him. "My dog's name is Maxine."

Celia stands up, pulls a chair over, and sits down. She starts signing into my hands. Again, I voice as she signs. "How..." My eyebrows shoot up in exhausted confusion. "O-L-D old is M-A-X-I-N-E Maxine, question mark." I turn to Liqin. "She's three. I've had her since she was two. That's when she graduated from guide dog school."

Celia starts signing.

My brain feels fried. Barbecued. Blasted. I can't process any more sign language.

I give Celia an apologetic look, then lift my hands off hers. "Liqin, can I show you something?" I gesture for him to come over to the table. When he stands by the table, I turn my braille computer so that the QWERTY keyboard faces him. "Type your question." He says something. I point at the keyboard. "I can't hear you, but if you type it I can read it." He starts typing. "When you're done, pass the computer back to me."

He hands me the computer. I turn it around so that the braille faces me. My fingers glide over the line of text: *how does this work?*

"When you hit a key, pins pop up to form braille letters," I respond aloud. "This is a braille computer called a BrailleNote. It's basically a computer with a tactile screen instead of a visual screen." I turn the computer around and push it toward him.

He types, then pushes the computer back to me. The text reads: *This computer is very cool. Oh, I think class is starting now, TTYL.*

I put my earbuds on. "Okay, class is starting. Who can tell me about [mumble mumble]."

My mind whirs with ideas. If I bring a wireless keyboard to class with me, then I could read as Liqin types, allowing me to respond in real-time. We wouldn't have to pass the computer back and forth. Maybe, just maybe, other students would talk to me, too.

*   *   *

Connecting with classmates and professors is important to me, but it's not the only reason I moved from Oregon to Massachusetts. My personal experiences with discrimination, as well as those I heard from others, sparked my desire to develop legal advocacy skills. My pre-law advisor urged me to strive for the highest ranked school so I could gain access to the most employment opportunities. Even lawyers with disabilities face employment discrimination.

After I spent months crafting a competitive law school application, offers came pouring in from all across the country. And then came the big one: Harvard Law School. Harvard offered me admission with a financial aid package that included grants and loans. Leaving the Best Coast for the East Coast didn't appeal to me, but I knew I had to do everything in my power to increase my chances of becoming a successful lawyer. My parents supported the move, especially after I promised to return to California post-graduation.

In some ways, Harvard feels a lot like my other schools. The written word serves as my lifeline through the learning process. The disability office works with professors to convert all written materials into an accessible format. Studying the reading materials and class notes has served me well in the past. I suspect it will work here, too. My biggest struggle will be finding a better way to communicate with classmates and professors.

Gordon braved a cross country move to join me in Cambridge. He started a small business here helping families, students, and organizations with their technology. He's really good with computers. He has solved problems for me that Harvard IT couldn't solve.

Earlier in the year I proposed creating a communication system by connecting a Bluetooth keyboard to my braille computer. Braille computers have been around for decades, their capabilities evolving over time. This year, HumanWare released the BrailleNote Apex, the very first BrailleNote with Bluetooth capabilities. The California Department of Vocational Rehabilitation purchased two of these computers for me to support my education and employment goals. Gordon and I paired the BrailleNote with several different Bluetooth keyboards, seeking the most portable, functional, and comfortable combination.

After class I meet up with Gordon at Asmara Restaurant in Central Square. The keyboard and braille computer are on the table between us. "I'm thinking about using this keyboard to talk with classmates." My left hand rests on the braille display, waiting for his response. My right hand reaches for my cup of cinnamon spice tea.

His words pop up on the braille display as he types, "How come you're not already using it in class?"

"Because..." I hesitate. I often suppress my worries because most people blow them out of proportion. Gordon listens to my concerns without exaggerating them, though, so I tell him. "People might think it's weird."

"This is 2010. Everybody types. There's nothing weird about typing."

"True...One of my classmates typed on the BrailleNote today. He said it was cool."

"It is cool! All someone has to do is hit a key and *voilà*! Braille. Other than the fact that it's in braille, it's just like texting and instant messaging."

I already know all of this; I'm the one who came up with the idea for this system. And yet... Sometimes lining up a series of known facts uncovers a hidden one. Gordon is reminding me, in his own kind way, to discard ableist and constraining ideas. "Thanks, I needed to hear that." While society expects lawyers to communicate in a certain way, I ultimately shape the type of lawyer I become.

Two weeks into the semester, I present my braille communication system at a meeting with Jody Steiner, the university's coordinator of Deaf and hard of hearing services; Cathleen Segal, the law school's director of disability services; and Jennifer Perrigo from the office of career services. The four of us have gathered around a conference table in Pound Hall. The law school has scheduled a workshop to help students master the art of networking, and I want to try using my braille communication system at the workshop.

"Let me make sure I have this straight." Jody speaks into the FM mic. "You're suggesting people would type on this keyboard and you would read it in braille?"

I nod.

"Okay, that sounds easy enough. Would you want to be sitting or standing?"

"What do people normally do at networking events?" I ask.

"I'll let Jen answer that. Passing this to Jen."

The mic changes hands. "We usually have people standing

and milling about. We'll have a few reception tables around the room. They're tall round tables."

"Let's plan to have this keyboard at one of the tables, then."

"Sure. We could certainly reserve a table for you and Jody. If you would rather sit, we could reserve chairs for you."

I shake my head. "I'm fine standing."

The mic moves again. "This is Jody. So you and I will be standing at one of these tall tables. The braille computer and keyboard will be on the table. How about Maxine? Where will she be? Will she have her own business cards?"

"So many cards! Everyone will know her name. I'll have her resting on the floor by my feet."

"Aww, Maxine. She's looking at me with those big, beautiful, brown, puppy dog eyes of hers. Okay," Jody continues, "I have a question for Jen. This is going to be a large room full of lawyers. I don't mean to stereotype lawyers, but...do you think people will come over to our table and type on the keyboard?"

The mic moves to Jen. "We reached out to people who have an interest in being mentors and helping young law students. I think this will be a good group. Jody's asking for the mic, so I'm going to pass it to her."

"Thanks, Jen. Haben, this question is for you. I think it's always good to plan ahead. Suppose someone spills wine on the keyboard. Heaven forbid, but accidents happen, you know? What do you think should be our backup plan?"

"Good point." I lean back in my chair, thinking. "I could carry a backup keyboard in my bag."

"Great! And if something happens to the braille computer?"

My nose wrinkles. "Those are expensive. I have a backup

braille computer at home, but I can't risk carrying both of them around. If a spill happens, it happens. There's always tactile sign language, though I only know the basics. So, tactile sign language is our Plan B."

"Got it. I'm sure it'll be just fine. You're going to rock this event! Cat, want to add anything? I'm passing the mic to Cat."

The mic moves again. "I'm sure you'll do great, Haben. If you think of anything else you need, just let us know. We're here for you."

On the day of the workshop, Jody leads me to our reserved table right in the middle of the room. I place the braille computer and keyboard on the tall round table.

"Is this working?" Jody types.

Nervousness has snatched my voice away, so I just nod.

"Yay! Okay, let's see. I'm looking around the room. There's a bar on the far left side of the room—a young man is there making drinks. Do you want a drink?"

I shake my head, no.

"Smart woman. Okay, more people are coming in. Behind you there's a table with two women chatting. Older, maybe in their fifties. To the left of them, so that's behind you and to the right, there are two guys and one woman. They're your age, so maybe students. Now they're walking over to the bar."

I clear my throat. "Do you think you could find people and bring them over?"

"Of course. Who do you want me to get?"

I shrug. "Anyone."

"Honey, that's too vague. I'm here to support you, and I

don't want my opinions to color your interactions. Give me clear instructions."

"Okay. Find someone who looks friendly."

"Define friendly."

I laugh nervously. "Let me think... see if you can spot someone who is smiling."

"Okay, I'm on it. Oh, about fifteen feet to my right, your left, there's a group of three guys. Well dressed, in their thirties, maybe? They're laughing and smiling about something. Want me to bring them over?"

"No!" My pulse starts racing. "I don't want to interrupt anyone. Let's avoid groups."

"Okay, so we're looking for smiling single people. Do you want me to tell you whether or not they're wearing a ring?"

"Jody!" A laugh ripples from my core to my fingers and toes. My shoulders finally relax. "Yes, go ahead, tell me everything!"

"Of course. Everyone else gets to see all these details. It's only fair that you get to know, too. If you want me to I can describe outfits, hairstyles, jewelry, facial expressions, you name it. You tell me what's important to you and I'll describe it."

"Okay." I flash her a delighted smile. "Do you see any people who are not in groups at the moment?"

"I'm looking... there's a guy standing near the drinks. Forties, maybe, but I can't see if he's smiling from here."

"Can you bring him over?"

"What do you want me to say?"

"You could say, 'Hi, may I introduce you to Haben? She'd like to meet you.' If he says yes, then explain to him, 'She's

Deafblind and uses a keyboard and braille computer. Come on over and I'll show you.' You can gesture to the table."

"Got it. BRB." Jody walks off into the big unknown.

I'm in the confounding position of being both ultra visible and invisible. People will stare—it's human nature. Eyes are drawn to people who stand out, like a black woman with a dog and strange computer in the middle of a Harvard Law School reception. People will judge—that's human nature, too. A lot of people will decide to avoid me, assuming I don't have anything of value to contribute. I can't control their actions, but I can control the messages I send.

My fingers find the keyboard on my computer. "You're confident," I type to myself. My fingers glide over the words, reading the message. Feel it. Think it. Believe it.

Two people approach the table. "It's Jody. Simon came over to say hello. He doesn't want to type, so I'm going to help him."

I extend my hand out to Simon. "It's nice to meet you, Simon. My name is Haben."

He shakes my hand, then holds it. I'm stuck reading with just one hand as he talks and Jody types for him. "Tell her it's a pleasure to meet her. What kind of dog is that? That's a gorgeous dog. Does the dog go to class with her? It must be smart. Well it was very nice meeting you both. She's very inspiring."

I cringe inwardly. People with disabilities get called inspiring so often, usually for the most insignificant things, that the word now feels like a euphemism for pity. Sometimes when a nondisabled person uses the word to describe a person with a disability, it's a sign that they're feeling overwhelmed or uncomfortable.

"This is probably a bit confusing." I slide my hand out of his grasp and gesture at the computer. "When you speak, Jody is typing what you're saying. What she's typing is then sent through Bluetooth to this braille computer. I'm then reading your words in braille. There's a slight delay between when you speak and when your words appear in braille. It might make more sense if you try typing. Would you like to try?"

"It's okay. I'm enjoying watching you two. This is my card. It was very inspiring meeting her. Tell her she's beautiful. You ladies take care." He walks away.

"It's just Jody now. I'm putting his card to the right of your computer. What did you think of that?"

"Hmm." Chin resting on my hand, I pretend to think. "That was . . . *inspiring*."

"Right?"

I nod, grinning. Coming into this event I was worried that something like this would happen. When a feared scenario actually occurs, its power weakens.

"Is there anything you want me to do differently next time?" Jody asks.

I shake my head. "Some people just won't take me seriously. There are people out there who will treat me with respect, though. Let's keep searching."

"I see a woman walking around. Thirties, holding a drink in one hand. Kind of smiling."

I nod. "Let's meet her."

"Okay, BRB." Jody walks away.

My knees balance my weight as I kneel beside Maxine. Stretched out on the floor by my feet, she exudes a Zen-like calm in this room full of fancy lawyers. I run my hands through her fur, hoping some of her tranquility transfers over to me.

Jody returns. "Haben, this is Sarah. She's going to type. I'm stepping back now. Here's Sarah."

I extend a hand to Sarah. "Nice to meet you, Sarah." She shakes my hand, then releases it.

"Hello," she types.

I give her an encouraging smile. "How's your evening going?"

"Good. Do I need to hit enter?"

I shake my head. "No need to hit enter. Everything you type comes through instantly. The letters come up in braille as soon as you press them."

"Wow! Can I feel it?"

I turn the device around so that the braille display faces her. She touches the line of braille. When she's done, I turn it back around to face me.

"That is so cool. Is this technology new?"

"This particular device came out this year, but there have been devices like this since the eighties. Do you work in tech?"

"Kind of. So, as you probably guessed, I'm a lawyer. I graduated from NYU Law five years ago."

"Awesome! What kind of law do you practice?"

"We do business law. My firm has an office in downtown Boston, and we'll be taking applications for summer associates soon. Are you interested?"

I take a moment to choose my words carefully. "That sounds like a great opportunity. I ultimately want to become a disability rights lawyer. Does anyone at your office handle civil rights cases?"

"I've done a few cases pro bono. I know someone else has, too. I want to give you my card so we can stay in touch. Do I give it to you or your interpreter?"

"Give it to me, please." A card appears in my hand. "Thanks. I really enjoyed meeting you, Sarah. I hope you have a great evening."

"You, too. Bye!" She picks up her drink and walks away.

"It's Jody. There's a student waiting to talk to you. Sweet smile. He says he knows you. Here he is."

"Hi, what's your name?" I ask.

"Hey, it's Liqin."

"Liqin! Hi! How's the reception going for you?" I'm smiling, thrilled to find a friend.

"I've met several interesting people, got some new business cards." His words zip by, double the speed of the last typist. "I'd say it's going pretty well. How about you?"

"I just had a nice conversation with a lawyer named Sarah. She was telling me about her firm's summer program."

"Awesome! I just wanted to say hi. There are only a few of us from our class at this event. BTW, the other day I was at the cafeteria and through the window I saw you playing ball with Maxine. It looked fun."

"Yeah, she loves to play! You can play with her sometime, too."

"Thanks, that would be great. I'll email you. Okay, I'm going to go meet more people. See you around."

"Bye!"

Jody continues to facilitate conversations throughout the evening. She types visual and audio descriptions, and then lets me make the decisions. I meet many people, both current law students and lawyers.

The experience energizes me, and I continue expanding my social circle. Classmates type on the keyboard before and after class; new acquaintances in coffee shops introduce themselves over the keys; and for the first time in my life, dance partners have an easy way to tell me their names. On rare occasions people walk away, or make dismissive comments. I tell Maxine to steer around them. Most people are thoughtful, inquisitive, and willing to try having conversations in a new way. The familiarity of the keyboard provides an opening that allows me to help people feel comfortable despite our differences. Most people don't know braille, sign language, or disability culture, but a significant number of people know how to type. Millennials in particular tend to have plenty of experience conversing through keyboards. In that way, the keyboard operates like a life raft people can cling to in a vast sea of unknowns.

Exploring my communication options only takes up a tiny fraction of my time, though. Most of my hours are spent reading textbooks, cases, and notes on those cases. The school sends me all my materials as digital files that I can access on my computer. Accessible documents, applications, and websites also allow me to conduct legal research and write papers. More tech developers are designing with access in mind, and that increases opportunities for students with disabilities. As a student in 2010, I have access to more study tools than many past students with disabilities. Disability rights advocates have been working to remove barriers for years, and their work has paved the way for students like me.

Harvard instructors assign an extraordinary amount of homework. It's daunting, but the work ethic I began to develop in middle school and honed throughout college serves me especially well now. I keep track of assignments, prioritize tasks, and seek advice from librarians, instructors, and experienced students. Both the Black Law Students and the Women Law Students associations save me during finals, offering mentors and study tips. The final exams are grueling. Exhausting. Brutal. The law school provides me the exams in braille, and a laptop with a screenreader and braille display for me to type and print out my answers. My exams, like all students' exams, will be graded anonymously.

After my last exam, an email rises out of my inbox to torment me with an impossible question: would I like to celebrate the end of finals with my classmates at a bar? Yes, I would. No, I would not. Yes. No. Bars have sticky tables and stickier floors. Bars are loud environments where I won't hear anyone, and no one will hear me.

The time has come for me to learn how to handle bars. Lawyers have gathered in bars since time immemorial. I mean, the final test to become a lawyer is called a *bar* exam.

Maxine and I walk from our off-campus apartment to the law school, cross through the law school, navigate our way across Harvard Yard, traverse Harvard Square, and enter the legendary John Harvard's Brewery & Ale House. The smells of beer and fried food greet us at the door. "Forward." We descend the stairs. "Good girl!" She pauses at the bottom of the stairs as if to say, "Now what?"

Through the dim light I see a crowd of people all around us.

215

To the front, to the left, to the right. The voices merge into one large cacophony of chaos.

A person approaches and touches my arm. She speaks, and her words fade into the noise.

"Hi!" I smile. "It's hard for me to hear. I want to set up my keyboard. Would you show me to a counter or table I can use?"

She leads me through the crowd of people to the tall wood surface of the bar.

"Thank you!" I pull the keyboard and braille display out of my bag, turn them on, and pass the keyboard to her.

"Hey, it's Janet. How are you?"

"Good! I'm relieved finals are over."

"Me, too. We made it! We survived!"

"They say everything will be easier now that we've finished our first semester." I feel giddy sitting here at a bar, sharing an ordinary conversation about school. Noisy settings always left me feeling lost and isolated in the past. I avoided them when I could—I skipped my high school's prom and my college grad-uation ceremony. Things are going to be different now that I know there are people who will respect me and my keyboard.

"Do you want anything to drink?" Janet asks.

I nod. "Lemonade."

"Okay, I'll tell the bartender. Liqin wants to say hi." Janet talks with the bartender, then disappears into the crowd.

A tall guy takes the keyboard. "Hey, it's Liqin. How did your finals go?"

"They were hard," I say with a shrug. "But I gave it my best. How about you?"

"That contracts exam was intense. I'm glad it's all over. I'm ready to go home for the holidays. Get away from HLS for a while. Your drink is here, just to your right."

My right hand reaches out and finds the drink. I take a sip.

"Is that lemonade?" he asks.

"Yes." I raise my eyebrows, wondering if he is going to tease me about my drink choices.

"No alcohol? Don't you want to celebrate?"

I smile. "I'm already Deafblind. I don't want to be Deaf, blind, and drunk."

"Hahahahahaha! That's funny. Well, it's your night to celebrate, too. Do you want anything else? Food?"

I shake my head. "Maybe you could describe the bar?"

"Sure! The bar is kind of L-shaped. We're halfway along the longer side of the L. People are sitting and standing all along this counter. They all look young. Probably all students celebrating the end of finals. I feel like I'm writing a scene in a book."

"Yes! Pretend you're a novelist, or a screenwriter."

"Hahaha. Let's see, what else... the entrance is on the left, that large wooden staircase you came down with Maxine. FYI, everyone was admiring her when you two walked in."

"Don't tell her," I warn darkly. "Her ego is already too big."

"Haha, she's perfect. Okay, so back to the descriptions: if you come down the stairs and turn right, you're in the restaurant, a large area with tables and booths. It's packed. Oh, Lisa just told me she's waiting to talk to you. I'll pass the keyboard to her. There are about twenty people from our section hanging out just behind you, so you can ask any one of us if you need anything. Are you good?"

"More than good!" I gesture for him to pass the keyboard.

"Awesome. Okay, here's Lisa."

The keyboard and braille display make hanging out at a bar easier than I expected. Throughout the evening, classmates come to appreciate how typing gives their vocal cords a break from shouting in the loud bar. My keyboard is like curb cuts on sidewalks in that nondisabled people find the accommodation useful, too. Disability solutions benefit the entire community.

A tall person moves in front of the keyboard. "Hey its me."

"Me who?" I ask.

"Oh rifgt sirry its Liqin I wsbt asj ig uiy meef aborjet dtomk."

My fingers try to decipher the message. "What?"

Gibberish.

If eyes can twinkle, mine are twinkling. "This is a tough question, a really hard question. How many drinks have you had?"

Gibberish.

"That's what I thought." I stifle a laugh.

A new person joins us at the bar. "Hey, it's Nick. What's up?"

I gesture toward Liqin on the other side of Nick. "He was trying to say something. Would you ask what he wanted to tell me?"

Nick turns to his left. Liqin leans into Nick's ear. Nick leans into Liqin's ear. They go back and forth. Then Nick returns to the keyboard. "He's asking if you need more lemonade?"

I point to my glass. "I actually haven't finished mine. That was nice of him to ask, though."

"His speech is pretty slurred."

"I'm not surprised." My face lights up with amusement. "He's been typing gibberish."

"Hahahaha! Hey, if there's anything you want to talk about you should ask me now before my typing skills go, too."

"That's right, you've all been drinking. Uh oh," I feign concern.

"BTW, I think Maxine has been drinking, too."

"What?!" My hands follow the leather leash to her soft furry head under the counter. Her nose investigates a spot on the floor. "No!" She lifts her nose off the floor. "Good girl." I sit back up and turn to Nick. "It's not safe for her to drink alcohol. Her liver is tiny, not like law students'."

"Haha. It was just a little spilled beer. I'll let you know if I see her licking the floor again."

"Thanks!"

"I'm heading out soon. Relax and have fun over the holidays. See you in January!"

"You, too. Bye!"

"Lisa is taking the keyboard now. Bye!"

The keyboard changes hands. "Hi, it's Lisa again. I don't mean to be rude, but why aren't you drinking? Nothing wrong with it, just wondering if it's a disability thing?"

"There are people with disabilities who drink. It's a personal choice for me." I lift my hands in a partial shrug. "I like having fine motor skills."

"LOL. Good point. I'm going to head home before I pass out. Do you need help getting home?"

"Nope. I know this area."

"You sure?"

"Yes."

"Okay. Most people have left the bar. Liqin is still here. Can I get a hug?"

We hug, and then Lisa leaves.

I reach for my glass. The cool drink soothes my throat. Talking over loud background noise has exhausted my voice. I wish I had set up a system with a visual display so I could type my side of the conversation, too. Or better yet, next time we could all hang out in a quieter environment.

"I'm heading out," I tell Liqin. "Are you doing okay?" I place the keyboard in front of him.

Gibberish.

My eyebrows furrow. "Are you going to be able to get yourself home?"

Gibberish.

If I were in his shoes, what would I want a friend to do? "I can walk with you. Your dorm is on my way home."

Gibberish.

I drum my fingers on the table. "Yeah, you should head home. We'll walk together. Come on, let's go." I pick up the keyboard and turn it off.

His hands clasp the keyboard. I pry it out of his hands. He reaches for it again.

"Okay, hang on." I switch the keyboard on and place it in front of him. "It's on now."

Gibberish.

I laugh. "I'm sorry! What you're typing isn't making sense. But it's much quieter outside. Tell me outside." I pack up my communication system and put my coat on.

Liqin stays seated at the bar. As I stand next to him, waiting for him to leave, my fingers absently trace the letters engraved on Maxine's leash: THE SEEING EYE.

Liqin reaches down and pets her.

I address Maxine with an enthusiastic, "Are you ready to go?!" She leaps up. Her tail swishes against my legs, wagging away as if to say, "Let's go, let's go, let's go!"

Liqin clambers out of his chair.

"Forward!" Maxine bolts for the stairs. "Slow down." As I step toward the stairs, I look back at Liqin. He lumbers along behind us. "Maxine, slow." We keep pace with Liqin as he mounts the stairs. Maxine stops at the door. I pull it open, then wait for Liqin to go through.

The past days of warmer winter weather have cleared the Cambridge streets of slippery snow and ice. Lucky for the students out drinking—lucky for Liqin.

"What did you want to tell me?" I ask.

Mumble, mumble.

I lean in closer. "What?"

Mumble, mumble.

"Sorry, I'm still not hearing you." I adjust my bag's shoulder strap. "I'm walking home, and your dorm is on my way. Want us to walk with you?"

Mumble, mumble.

"Follow me." Maxine and I reposition ourselves. "Maxine, forward. Good girl!" We walk down Dunster Street toward Harvard Square. Liqin stays behind us, muttering as he walks. He has a halting, zigzagging walk. Maxine and I slow down to match his speed.

The sidewalk widens into the open plaza of Harvard Square. Halfway across the square, Liqin turns right, shuffling off in the wrong direction.

Maxine and I hurry after him. When we catch up, I tug at his arm. "Your dorm is the other way."

No response.

"Maxine and I are going left." I point to the left.

"Maxine?" he asks.

"Yeah!" I look down at my dog and ask with exuberance, "Maxine, are you ready to go?" Her tail swishes against my legs. As Maxine moves, Liqin follows. The three of us walk together through Harvard Square. Soon we enter Harvard Yard, an enormous grassy field dotted with brick buildings and surrounded by brick walls. A confusing array of paved paths crisscross the Yard. Maxine strides through with confidence, picking out the right path.

Liqin shambles off the path.

"Liqin!" I call after him. Maxine and I catch up. "Would it help you if you hold my arm?" I lift his left hand and put it around my right elbow.

Mumble, mumble. His hand drops to his side.

"Can you try to stay with us? Follow Maxine, okay?"

Mumble, mumble.

Liqin follows Maxine through Harvard Yard, around the Science Center, and past the Langdell Law Library. Maxine and I drop him off at his dorm, safe and sound. That was my plan, anyway.

In actuality, what happens is this: Liqin follows Maxine through Harvard Yard, around the Science Center, and along the Langdell Law Library. Then he stops, catapults up the library steps, and sits.

A surprised laugh escapes my mouth. I gaze at the silhouette on the stairs, wondering what to do.

This is the guy who reached across the unknowns of disability—the technology, the interpreters, the watchful dog—to start a conversation with me. Now our roles have reversed. This time I'm the one reaching into the unknown. How on Earth will I get him to come down and go home?

Maxine and I mount the steps. I sit down beside Liqin and adopt an upbeat tone. "It's Haben and Maxine. I have some good news. You finished your finals."

Mumble, mumble.

"You're done. You're free. You don't have to live in the library."

Mumble, mumble.

"You're really close to your dorm. Don't you want to go home?"

Mumble, mumble.

I feel stuck—stuck on these cold, hard stairs, stuck outside on this wintry night. I run my hands through Maxine's fur, trying to warm them. Liqin starts petting her, too. That gives me an idea.

"Maxine is heading that way. Come on." I stand up and address Maxine, using the same cheery voice I've used all evening. "Are you ready to go?" Maxine and I descend the stairs, but Liqin remains seated. I wait at the bottom, hoping he'll come down on his own.

He hollers, "Maxine!"

I address my dog again, talking loud enough for Liqin to hear. "Maxine, are you ready to go?" The whole harness shakes as she wags her tail. Maxine and I start walking. Behind us, Liqin finally gets up, clambers down the stairs, and makes the short trek from the library to his dorm. Maxine and I travel another block to our apartment off campus.

My first semester of law school bestowed many valuable lessons, and the most memorable one is this: hold off on the drinks in case a friend needs help getting home.

I'm the first Deafblind student at Harvard Law School. Harvard excluded many groups throughout its history. When Helen Keller was applying for college, Harvard wouldn't admit her. Back in those days, Harvard only admitted men. Helen's disability didn't hold her back, nor did her gender; it was the community at Harvard that chose to create barriers for women. Harvard's sister school, Radcliffe College, offered Helen Keller admission, and she received her degree in 1904.

The Harvard community chose to exclude women for the first two hundred–plus years of its existence. Over time, the culture shifted. Adapted. Changed. Harvard eventually opened its doors to women, people of color, and people with disabilities.

Harvard has come a long way since Helen's time, and there is still more work to do.

Throughout my three years at Harvard Law School, I continue to face challenges. The school doesn't know exactly which accommodations I need. Neither do I—doing law school Deafblind is new to me, too. We engage in an interactive process. We try different strategies, one after another, until we find the right solutions. I pass all my classes, even earning several honors. Over the summer, I gain valuable work experience—first at the U.S. Department of Education Office for Civil Rights, then at the U.S. Equal Employment Opportunity Commission. In my final year I'm honored with a Skadden Fellowship, one of the most prestigious fellowships in the legal field. The Skadden Foundation will provide two years of financial support for my work to increase access to digital reading services for blind students. I'll be working at Disability Rights Advocates, a nonprofit law firm in Berkeley, California.

No more cold, snowy winters for us. "Maxine, are you ready to go?"

Chapter Twenty-Three

Kicking Butt, Legally Speaking

Burlington, Vermont. Winter 2015.

Disability rights hero Daniel Goldstein grips the court's attention. He stands at the lectern before Judge William K. Sessions III in the United States District Court for the District of Vermont. Dan leads the oral arguments while attorneys Mehgan Sidhu, Greg Care, Emily Joselson, James DeWeese, and I analyze every word from our positions at the plaintiffs' counsel table.

Behind us, blind individuals and sighted allies sit listening to the debate that will affect our access to books. Heidi Viens, the lead plaintiff, is a blind mother who lives in Colchester, Vermont. She loves reading to her four-year-old daughter. If we win, Heidi and other blind readers would gain access to a library of over forty million books and documents.

Our team also represents the National Federation of the Blind (NFB), the oldest and largest organization led by blind people. With chapters in every state, the NFB has more than fifty thousand members. The organization has devoted an extensive amount of resources to teaching the public about accessibility. The NFB website offers an array of guides and tools on making information accessible. Despite the volume and accessibility of all this valuable information, numerous organizations ignore these suggestions. So the NFB employs a team of lawyers to protect the rights of blind Americans.

About a year ago, I received complaints from blind people experiencing access barriers on Scribd. The San Francisco based company built a publishing platform and digital library advertised as "the world's largest collection of e-books and written works." Blind people trying to read books in the Scribd library hit a wall. The company programmed the library in a way that blocks screenreaders, software that converts visual information on screen to speech or digital braille.

When I told NFB about the complaints coming in regarding Scribd, they were appalled. The Scribd situation struck a sensitive chord, especially because increasing access to books for children and adults is a core part of NFB's mission. Digital barriers hinder our education and employment opportunities, and limit our participation in the marketplace of ideas.

We sent Scribd a letter describing the access barriers and inviting them to work with us to fix the problems—no response. We sent the letter again—no response. We waited and waited. No response ever came.

So, bright and early on my twenty-sixth birthday, we sued them.

Scribd's lawyer called for the court to throw out our case. In its motion to dismiss for failure to state a claim, Scribd argued that the Americans with Disabilities Act (ADA) does not cover internet-based businesses. Title III of the ADA prohibits discrimination by a "place" of public accommodation. The word "place," Scribd alleged, means a physical location; spaces like restaurants, hotels, and movie theaters. Pointing out that it doesn't have a physical "place" open to the public, Scribd said it didn't have to make its library accessible.

My team disagreed. Strongly. Vehemently. I volunteered to write our brief opposing Scribd's motion to dismiss. Drafting that document was one of the most exciting moments of my legal career, almost as exciting as writing the complaint against Scribd. Writing is advocacy. Writing is strength. Writing is power. My years of practicing persuasive writing, legal research, and analytical reasoning poured into this one brief. When we finished, our team leader Dan Goldstein praised it as one of the best briefs he'd ever seen.

Now, Dan stands before the court to voice the arguments from our brief and address the court's questions. He's a skilled orator, with decades of experience litigating on behalf of blind people. Dan believes that blind people, with the right tools and training, can compete on equal footing with our sighted counterparts. Dan himself is a person with disabilities, living with both depression and anxiety disorders. He has generously given his time to mentoring many young disability rights lawyers, including me.

Typists transcribe the proceedings, sending the words to me in braille. Sitting with my colleagues at the plaintiffs' counsel table, I feel the exhilaration of my disability rights work culminating in this courtroom. If the court agrees with Scribd, blind Americans will lose access to Scribd's library of over forty million books and documents. A Scribd victory might even cause other tech companies to slash accessibility from their agenda— a disaster that would widen the digital divide.

It all comes down to this question: does the law consider the internet a "place?"

Dan: When you look at common usage, we can't talk about the internet without using the language in place. We visit a website. We don't "visit" a television station or a newspaper. We listen to or watch the television station, and we read the newspaper, but we visit a website. When the *Burlington Free Press* tells those who want to know how to help rebuild the Green Mountain Club in the wake of a fire to "visit" the club's website, I don't think the *Burlington Free Press* is being poetic and metaphorical. That's the language we all understand. We don't speak of cyber. We speak of cyber "space." We talk in chat "rooms." We post news on Facebook "walls." We have email "addresses." We shop at online "stores." When the *Times Argus* says in 2001 the internet is not just a place but lots of places, again I don't think they are being metaphorical. That's language. We all understand it and we understand it the first time we hear it. We understand "website." That's a web "place" in the common understanding of the word "site" ...

Court: That may be the common meaning, but the problem with that argument is that this statute was passed in

1990. The question is what did place mean at the time of the passage of the statute in the first place, and if in fact Congress at that point felt that there should be this physical property threshold to the application of the ADA, then they must have been talking about something other than the internet. They must have been talking about some physical building location.

Dan: If they were, then again the question is...why then do they abandon the word "place" in the oddest places? They use "establishment" instead of "place." They define "public accommodation" but not "place of public accommodation," although the regulations do, and I'll address that in a minute. Why don't they use it in the heading of the statute that is the core of Title III defining what's prohibited? And it's because place is not an operative word. It's a descriptive word. And one way to see that is when you try to change, for example, "a bakery, grocery store, clothing store, hardware store, shopping center, or other sales or rental establishment." If you want to use "place" you have to say "or other place." I think you have to say "or other place where sales or rentals occur," or something. I mean, it's too clunky. They weren't trying to— to limit something. They were just trying, whether they used "place" or "establishment," to describe something. And they used it over and over again when they are saying "or other" to make it as broad as they knew how to do using the English language. And knowing that they lived in an age of technology where, which they acknowledge

230

in the statutory history, which was going to affect the
way the ADA worked ...

How surreal to actually be here, witnessing this monumental
debate, after working on these issues for years! These arguments have occupied space in my thoughts even before I wrote
our Scribd complaint back in 2014. During my last year of
law school, I wrote two papers that addressed the application
of the ADA to online businesses. Now for the last year I've
been embroiled in this Scribd saga: does the ADA cover virtual
"places?"

The ADA is one of America's most comprehensive civil rights
laws. Republicans and Democrats joined forces to pass the bill
through Congress. Republican President George H. W. Bush
signed the bill into law on July 26, 1990. Opponents immediately began chipping away at the ADA. Defense attorneys
jabbed long and hard at the word "place," creating a hole for
their clients to slip through. Those cases set the precedent for
the idea that the ADA does not cover websites and apps.

Inaccessible websites and apps accelerate the information
famine. People who have visual disabilities, dyslexia, and other
print-reading disabilities face economic hardships spurred by
the lack of access to job applications, health notices, government forms, and educational materials. Technology has the
potential to remove barriers, but developers keep designing inaccessible digital services.

The U.S. District Court for the District of Massachusetts
was the first court to hold that the ADA covers internet-based
businesses. The National Association of the Deaf sued Netflix

for failing to provide captions for its online video streaming services. Captions—text that appears on screen—allow Deaf people to access the audio content of videos. Netflix argued that the ADA does not cover virtual businesses. Judge Ponsor disagreed, ruling that the ADA does in fact cover virtual businesses like Netflix. That 2012 Netflix case marked a new era for accessibility advocates.

When Dan finishes speaking, Scribd's attorney takes the lectern before Judge Sessions. Tonia Ouellette Klausner works for the behemoth Wilson, Sonsini, Goodrich & Rosati. Based in the firm's New York City office, Tonia's extensive work defending companies has earned her a spot on the list of "New York Super Lawyers." On top of that, she also went to school in Vermont.

Court: Do you know what happened to Judge Ponsor's case, the Netflix case? It was in 2012, so was it appealed?

Tonia: No. Netflix settled the case.

Court: Okay.

Tonia: Which is unfortunate we don't have the benefit of the First Circuit weighing in on here.

Plaintiffs argue that while Scribd does operate equipment and equipment falls within the definition of facilities—if I can just use their chart here, their quote from the statute, what the Department of Justice has said—it's not just that a business has to operate a facility or operate equipment. If it did, every single business in America would be covered by Title III. That may be what Plaintiffs would like, but that's not what the statute says and that's not what the regulations say. It has to be a place of public accommodation, which means a facility. So, it has to be a facility. It has to be physical; somebody operating equipment or a building, but that facility has to fall within—and fall within at least one of the twelve categories listed in the ADA.

There are two parts to the test. It has to be a place, a facility, and it has to fall within one of those categories. And a subscription reading service, an online publisher, doesn't fall within any of those categories. It hasn't for years…

Court: What they are basically suggesting is that the computer is the equipment, i.e. the facility, and based upon that they are providing library services—because, I mean essentially, you're an online library, aren't you?

Tonia: No. It's not a library. You don't check out books. You don't go in and peruse things. It is a—the Plaintiffs in their complaint characterize it as a subscription reading service and an online publication platform.

Court: Well, okay. All right.

Tonia: All right. Thank you.

Court: Thank you. Okay. Thank you and appreciate very much your coming today and I will take it under advisement.

Maxine jumps to her feet, pulling me out of the world of words. The floor and table shift as people pack up. My pulse is still racing with adrenaline. Did we convince the court? Will the judge classify Scribd as a "place" of public accommodation?

My co-counsel Mehgan pulls the keyboard over and types, "We're going to meet up at the Farmhouse to debrief."

I nod. "That's a nice one. I had lunch there yesterday."

"Do you want to walk there together?"

"Yeah. I just want to take a few minutes to thank the typists. Then I want to stop by the bathroom. Then I want to let Maxine use the bathroom. Actually"—I give her an apologetic smile—"would it be okay if I meet you there?"

"Of course. Take your time. We'll save you a seat."

The thank-yous and farewells take a while, and half an hour goes by before I finally leave the courthouse. My California winter coat staves off just a sliver of the biting Burlington cold. Maxine "parks" in the snow, then hops back up on the sidewalk. My right hand holds her leash while my left hand holds the arm of my friend Cameron Lash. We met in Boston when she was training to become an interpreter. She is a gifted communicator who brings joy everywhere she goes. She recently facilitated communication for me in Ethiopia where I keynoted several disability rights celebrations, garnering support for the Tsehay Zewde Memorial Scholarship for blind women attending college. Cameron also joined me in China where I met with disability rights leaders and gave a lecture at Renmin University's Law School in Beijing. Now Cameron is in Vermont on a different kind of disability rights mission.

As we walk through downtown Burlington, I ask Cam, "You know at the end when Scribd's lawyer was arguing that Scribd is not a library?"

"Kind of. But honestly Haben, it's all a bit of a blur. I was just trying to type as fast as I can."

"You did great! I just have a small question about tone and body language. At the very end, Scribd's attorney was claiming, again, that Scribd is not a library. The judge responded, 'Okay. All right.' Do you remember his tone? Was it like a skeptical, 'Okay, all right,' or was it—"

Cameron squeezes my arm. My heart rate rockets into high alarm. She continues walking. I walk beside her in silence.

A minute later, Cameron's body relaxes. "That was him!"

I gasp. "The judge?"

"Yes! He was walking in front of us!"

"Do you think he heard me?" My face grows hot.

"I don't know...I don't think so. He was about thirty feet ahead, walking on a sidewalk going perpendicular to us."

"Okay." I take a deep breath.

"What were you asking me?"

Sifting through my thoughts, I discover the question has faded. "I was asking you about the judge's tone and facial expressions, but now I feel like that's not important. The words are enough. We'll find out what he thinks when he publishes his opinion."

"How long until it's published?" Cam asks.

"There isn't a specific date." I shrug. "A few weeks to a few months."

"Wowzer."

I smile. "Yeah."

Two weeks later, I sit working at my desk in a warm California office. Sunlight pours in through floor-to-ceiling windows. They give Maxine an unobstructed view of the birds and squirrels enjoying Berkeley's Martin Luther King Jr. Civic Center Park.

When my parents visited my office, they clucked at the bare walls, instructing me on what to put up. One wall now has a scarf decorated with Ethiopian coffee scenes. Dr. Tedros, Ethiopia's Minister of Foreign Affairs, presented it to me. The scarf serves as a light, silky reminder of our recent trip to Ethiopia. Another wall displays my Harvard Law degree. My parents don't understand exactly what I do—"Something to do with disabilities." They don't understand exactly why I'm not rich. But they understand that I'll be okay.

As a public service lawyer, my salary is far below what a Harvard Law graduate would typically make, but still exceeds the average income for blind Americans, seventy percent of whom struggle with unemployment. The Harvard Low Income Protection Plan supports my public service work by subsidizing part of my student loans. In a society that casts people with disabilities as inferior to the nondisabled, having a meaningful job, health insurance, and a law degree feels like a privilege. So I spend hours at my desk working to dismantle our world's barriers.

An email announces new activity in the Scribd case. Judge Sessions made his decision! Heart pounding, I begin to read:

UNITED STATES DISTRICT COURT
FOR THE
DISTRICT OF VERMONT

NATIONAL FEDERATION   :
OF THE BLIND, on behalf   :
of its members and itself,   :
and HEIDI VIENS,   :
      Plaintiffs,   :
                    : Case No. 2:14-cv-162

   v.   :
SCRIBD INC.,   :

                 :
      Defendant.   :

                 :

Opinion and Order

Plaintiffs National Federation of the Blind ("NFB") and Heidi Viens, a member of NFB residing in Colchester, Vermont, brought this suit against Scribd, Inc. ("Scribd"). The Plaintiffs' Complaint alleges that Scribd has violated Title III of the Americans with Disabilities Act ("ADA"), 42 U.S.C. § 12182, because its website and mobile applications ("apps") are inaccessible to the blind.

Scribd has moved to dismiss the Complaint with

prejudice pursuant to Federal Rule of Civil Procedure 12(b)(6) for failure to state a claim. ECF No. 13. Scribd argues that the Plaintiffs have not alleged facts demonstrating that it owns, leases, or operates a place of public accommodation because the ADA does not apply to website operators whose goods or services are not made available at a physical location open to the public. The Court disagrees. For the reasons discussed below, the Court denies Scribd's motion to dismiss.

I leap out of my chair and drop down to the floor. "Maxine, we won!"

She lifts her head and points her magnificent shepherd ears.

The court ruled that the ADA does in fact cover internet-based businesses. Deciding otherwise would lead to absurd results, like excluding services provided door-to-door or over the phone. Many companies provided services over the phone or door-to-door in 1990 when Congress passed the ADA, and Congress expected the statute to cover these "places." The court affirmed that Congress intended for the ADA to be a broad statute that evolves with technology. "Now that the Internet plays such a critical role in the personal and professional lives of Americans, excluding disabled persons from access to covered entities that use it as their principal means of reaching the public would defeat the purpose of this important civil rights legislation."

National Federation of the Blind v. Scribd is the first case in the Second Circuit to hold that the ADA covers online businesses, and the second case in the entire country. We've broken ground, set legal precedent, and made history. The court's decision will send a strong message to online businesses around the country: make websites and apps accessible, or else.

Accessibility is not only mandated by law, it's also good business. People with disabilities are the largest minority group. There are more than fifty-seven million Americans with disabilities, and there are more than 1.3 billion people with disabilities around the world. Organizations that design with disability in mind gain access to this gigantic market. Removing barriers also gives employers the opportunity to tap into a significant talent pool.

Guidelines—which are free and easy to find—exist to teach developers how to make websites and apps accessible. The Web Content Accessibility Guidelines, Android accessibility guidelines, and Apple accessibility guidelines are just a few. Despite conventional belief, computer programs are not inherently visual. Computer programs start as 1's and 0's. Developers have the power to convert those 1's and 0's into engaging applications that everyone can access.

As my hands pet Maxine's soft ears, my mind tallies all the things I now need to do: share the good news with our clients, draft a case update, collaborate with my team on next steps...The next stage of the case is discovery, and then the trial. There is a good chance Scribd will decide to settle. Defendants in ADA cases tend to settle after losing the motion to dismiss. The prospect of facing months or years of expensive litigation makes defendants realize that they'd save money, and win customers, if they just choose inclusion. We'll see what Scribd decides.

In the meantime, today's court decision calls for a celebration.

Chapter Twenty-Four

The White House ADA
Celebration

Washington, DC. Summer 2015.

"Now we're in the East Room!" Cameron and I have just walked into a spacious room in the White House. "Let's see...there's a small stage with a podium. It has the presidential seal in front, and a U.S. flag just behind it."

"Wow, the presidential seal." My pulse speeds up just thinking about it. "I wonder if I'll be speaking at that podium..."

"Haben Girma, are you nervous?"

"No way," I say automatically. Then I consider my emotions. She's right. I'm feeling nervous, but my heart is thumping with excitement, too. "Do you see anyone who looks like they work here?"

Cameron's body shifts as she scans the room. "There are two people on the right having a discussion. One of them has a clipboard."

"A clipboard? The White House really needs to upgrade their tech."

"Want to tell her?"

I laugh. "Sure!"

We cross the room. Cameron facilitates the conversation. "This woman says, 'You look familiar. Are you the introducer?'"

Smiling, I nod. "What's your name?"

"I'm Sally. We're really happy to have you here. If there is anything you need, you just let me know."

"Would it be okay if I go on stage and check out the podium?"

"You don't need to worry about that. We have someone who will walk you on and off the stage."

I gesture to Cam. "This is Cameron. She's going to walk on and off stage with me."

"I'm sorry," Sally says. "We actually can't do that. Our person will go with you."

My stomach drops. The need to advocate is ceaseless, even among family, even at a disability rights event. Taking a deep breath, I start again. "I'm Deafblind and need someone who can facilitate communication and provide visual descriptions. Cameron has experience working with me. She's facilitated communication in all kinds of environments, from Ethiopia to China. Does your person have training working with Deafblind people?"

"I understand what you're saying, but we have a protocol we need to follow," Sally explains.

"Oh, is it for security reasons? How about having both of them go up with me?"

"She's not authorized to go on stage. I'm really sorry."

I can feel the air being squeezed out of my lungs. The tension builds as my mind searches for a solution. All while the clock ticks forward, moving closer and closer to our start time.

I switch tactics. "Where is this person? Maybe I can train them. Can you introduce us?"

"Sure, let me get him."

We follow Sally into an adjacent room. Cameron shows me a table, and I slide the braille computer off my aching wrist. Cam writes, "Sally's on the other side of the room talking to a tall guy in a military uniform. Oh my word! Haben, I don't even know what to say. How the heck are you? Wait, they're coming over. His name is Ryan. I'm passing him the keyboard."

Cameron steps back from the table, and Ryan takes her place at the keyboard. "Hi!"

The exclamation mark makes me smile. "Nice to meet you, Ryan. It looks like you've figured out how this works. The keyboard is connected to the braille computer through Bluetooth. Everything you type comes through instantly. Don't worry about spelling or punctuation."

"Okay. Does it autocorrect?"

"I'm used to reading through typos, so my mind autocorrects."

"That's impressive."

"Thanks." I smile. "Let's talk about guiding. The main thing to remember is to lead with your body. Some people grab my arm and try to pull me. That's disempowering. Instead, offer your arm. That respects my right to choose. Make sense?"

"Yes."

"Great. You can touch your arm to mine and I'll know what

you mean. If I decide to let you lead, I'll hold your arm just above your elbow. Your elbow is connected to your shoulder, which is ultimately connected to your core. So when you walk, turn, or stop, I'll be able to feel it through your arm."

"Okay. Just so you know, there are a few steps going up to the stage and coming down from it," Ryan types.

"I'll be able to feel when your body moves up or down. You can also signal by touching my hand. I'll show you. Can we go on stage and practice?"

"Sure. Do I bring the keyboard?"

"I'll take that." I stack the keyboard on top of the braille computer, then carry both in my right arm.

Ryan moves to my left. He's taller than I expected, so I hold his arm just below his elbow. He heads to the East Room at a good pace, not the usual slow shuffle of first-time guiders. "By the way, if the path is ever too narrow for both of us to walk side-by-side, you can communicate by putting your arm behind you." Gently, I move his arm behind his back and step behind him. "That tells me we need to walk single file." Guiding his arm back to his side, I move back to his right side. "Try to convey environmental information the way a dancer expresses music." Ryan's arm arcs to the left as he turns. "Exactly!" His left hand touches my left hand, the one holding his arm. I feel for the first step with my foot, then walk up the steps. A moment later we're at the podium where I set up the keyboard and braille computer. "You did great, Ryan. Do you have any questions for me?"

"Would it be okay if I walk on your right side?"

I give him a quizzical look. "Sure... Why?"

"It will make it easier for the audience to see you."

"Oh..." I'm surprised and touched by his suggestion. "That's really thoughtful. Yeah, let's do that. Do you know where I'm supposed to go after my speech?"

"Yes, we'll exit on the right, go down the steps, and then you can stand there during the president's speech. Do you want a chair?"

I smile. "Yes, please. It's hard to read while standing. Cameron and Michael will be typing the speech, so they'll need chairs, too. Can we reserve three chairs?"

"Sure. I'll let them know."

"Great. Thanks, Ryan. I think we're all set. Let's walk off the stage." Collecting the keyboard and computer, I cradle my tech in my left arm. Ryan switches to my right side, and together we leave the stage.

Cameron and I congregate around a cocktail table near the door. "How did it go?" she asks.

"Shrug." I voice the word, playfully giving Cameron a visual description as I raise my shoulders and drop them. "No, actually, he did great. He seems really thoughtful. But the point of having someone experienced is that they would know what to do when the unexpected happens. I'm confident we'll do great as long as everything goes smoothly. But if something bizarre happens..."

"I'll help if I notice anything. I'll even come on stage if I have to."

"Cam!" My face breaks into an amused grin as I tell myself she's just joking.

"Well, what are they going to do?"

I laugh nervously. "Let's not find out."

"Did Ryan tell you what he does?"

I shake my head no.

"He has a badge that looks like a pair of wings." She draws the shape on the back of my hand. "I'm not a hundred percent sure, but I think that's the Air Force symbol."

"Oh…What do Airmen do at the White House? Could he be Secret Service? I'll have to ask him."

"So mysterious! Let me know when you find out."

I nod. "What are people up to now?"

"Most people are down the hall by the food. Chatting. Taking pictures. I see a few people with wheelchairs, canes, people signing…"

"Let's go meet them!"

The White House celebration of the twenty-fifth anniversary of the Americans with Disabilities Act has brought together advocates from all across the nation, including Rosemarie Garland-Thomson, a disability rights professor from Emory University, and the author of many texts on disability politics; Claudia Gordon, the former disability advisor for President Obama and the first Deaf African American woman to become an attorney; and Tom Harkin, a former senator from Iowa who championed passage of the ADA. I feel starstruck around all these heroes who paved the way for Generation ADA.

"Hey, Maria!" I give her a hug. Maria Town serves as the senior associate director for the Office of Public Engagement and a liaison for the disability community. She's also a good friend. "Congratulations on such a great event."

"Thanks! I can't really talk right now, but you need to go to the Red Room."

I laugh. More White House orders! "Okay, talk to you later."

"Wait, where's Maxine?"

"She's at home." Guilt stabs through my heart. "When people meet me, the conversation tends to focus on Maxine. Normally that's fine, but there's a chance I might get a minute with the president, and I want that minute to be about disability rights, not dogs."

"Interesting. I see what you're saying. Hey, I'm sorry, they're calling me. Go to the Red Room!"

"Going! Bye!"

In the Red Room, we discover about thirty guests waiting to meet the president and take a photo. People will line up in the Red Room, meet the president in the Blue Room, then wait for the speeches to start in the East Room. As their introducer, they want me to go last.

Cameron and I settle into a sofa, ready for a long wait, a wait that actually started a week ago when I received the invitation. Then three days ago, the White House invited me to introduce President Obama at the reception—they gave me twenty-four hours to write my speech. Friends listened and offered feedback as I practiced the speech over the weekend. My fingertips have run over the speech so many times that the words feel engraved on them. Now the words run through my head again as we wait in the Red Room.

"Valerie says she wants to say hi," Cameron types. "Valerie Jarrett, here she is!" Cam stands up and vanishes out of sight.

Valerie Jarrett is a senior advisor for the president who oversees the Office of Public Engagement and Intergovernmental Affairs. She sits on the sofa and places the keyboard on her lap. "Hi Haben, it's wonderful to meet you."

"It's wonderful to meet you, Valerie. It's a huge honor for me to be here. I'm kind of new, but some of the advocates here have been working on these issues for years, and their advocacy created more opportunities for the younger generation."

"Yes, we have a lot of amazing advocates here today. I've heard great things about your work, too."

"Thanks." I smile, touched by her kind words. "My specific focus is on technology. A lot of companies are building websites and apps that aren't accessible. The lack of accessible information online has created an information famine, putting people with disabilities at a disadvantage. We need more companies to realize that the ADA applies to digital services."

"We're very proud of what you're doing. Maria has told us about your work."

"Maria is amazing!"

"Yes she is! Do exclamation marks come through?"

"Yes, all punctuation comes through." I explain how the keyboard works.

"What if I make a typo?"

I give her a playful smile. "You, make a mistake?"

"I'm laughing!"

Sitting beside her, I can feel her amusement traveling through the sofa in gentle waves. Feeling her genuine laughter tells me that we've leapt over the typical disability awkwardness, and the realization leaves me beaming. "My goal is to connect with people given the tools and abilities we have. Typos don't matter because ninety-five percent of the time I can figure out what people mean."

"Thank you, Haben."

"I'm wondering..." I lean in to whisper. "Does the president know how to type?"

"Yes, he can type. Though maybe not as well as me."

My cheeks hurt as I laugh with delight, and I struggle to keep a hand on the computer.

"Ask him."

I stop laughing. "Are you sure? He won't get offended?"

"Not at all. He likes a challenge."

I nod. "You're right. I like being challenged, too. Thanks for reminding me to live boldly."

Valerie leaves the sofa, and Cameron sits back down. "It's Cam. When Valerie gave me the keyboard she had the biggest smile. She said, 'What a joy.'"

My heart melts. "She was really, really kind. I feel more confident after talking to her."

"Oh, good. You're going to need it."

I give her a quizzical look.

"Breaking news: while you were talking to Valerie, Sally came over to me. She said, 'Joe Biden is joining the event. Tell Haben to include him in her speech.'"

My jaw drops.

"I know!!! She said it like it was no big deal."

My shoulders shake with laughter. "All right, I'll add him to my speech. Give me a few moments of silence to think this through."

"Surely. Not a peep from me. If I see anything interesting I just won't tell you. Kidding! Don't worry, you know I—"

I lift my hands off the computer and cross my arms. Her elbow nudges me. My arm nudges her back, inducing stress-relieving laughter.

Leaning back in the sofa, I run my speech through my mind. Hmm, what order does one read the names? Normally people name the president before the vice president, right? Please welcome President Barack Obama and Vice President Joe Biden. What if people start clapping when they hear the president's name, drowning out the rest of my sentence? I signal the end of a speech by placing vocal stress on the last words. If I introduce the president first, the sentence will force me to place more emphasis on the vice president's name. Is that okay? I could reverse them. Please welcome Vice President Joe Biden and President Barack Obama. That would allow me to place more emphasis on the president's name, cueing the audience to applaud.

My fingers settle back on the computer. "Okay, I'm back. What did I miss?"

"Joe Biden is here! He's on the other side of the room with a crowd around him. He's smiling, shaking hands, looks like he's having a good time. Michael is sitting across from me. We've been chatting since you RUDELY cut me off!"

"Cam!" I laugh, grateful for her warm, playful presence. "Get ready, you're getting cut off again. Pass the keyboard to Michael."

"Fine!" Cam passes the keyboard.

I wave at Michael and sign, "How are you?" Sign language

lessons have improved my signing skills, but I'm still not fluent. My expressive signing is stronger than my receptive signing, so Deaf friends meet me halfway by typing their side of the conversation while I sign my side.

Michael Stein heads a disability rights law firm here in Washington, DC. He went through Harvard Law School and the Skadden Fellowship program several years before me. When I need advice from an experienced Deaf lawyer, he's the friend to whom I turn. Today, he'll be typing the president's speech for me, taking turns on the keyboard with Cameron.

"I'm doing great," Michael says. "Did Cameron tell you Joe Biden's here?"

I nod yes.

"Do you want to meet him?"

Doubts swirl through my mind. He's busy. He doesn't have time. I can't compete with the crowd...I tell Michael, "Yes, I want to meet him."

"Okay. I'll go get him." Michael passes the keyboard to Cameron.

"Cam," I whisper. "He said he's going to get Joe Biden!"

"Yup. He's walking over there now."

My heart starts pounding, nerves making my arms feel weak.

Then I remember cool, calm, confident Valerie Jarrett sweeping in to offer sage advice just when I needed it most. The memory of that conversation gives me a boost of self-assurance.

Cameron types, "Ryan is asking if you're ready." My eyebrows shoot up. "Don't look at me! I'm just the messenger. Here's Ryan."

He sits down with the keyboard. "Are you ready?"

"Probably." I smile. "Ready for what, exactly?"

"We should get in line. To meet the president."

"Oh! Yes, of course." Standing up, I transfer the braille computer from my lap to my arm. Ryan leads the way toward the door. We stop. We wait, and wait, and wait. "Ryan, can you give the keyboard to Cameron?"

"Hey, it's Cam. Thank you for getting me the keyboard!!!!!!!!!! I was staring at it trying to figure out how to steal it from Mr. Secret Service. Have you asked him what exactly he does?"

Biting down a laugh, I shake my head no.

"Interesting. Well, you let me know if you find out anything about that one. By the way, I'm standing at a table to your eleven o'clock. There are about four people in front of you in line. I peeked into the Blue Room and I saw Obama!!!! He's wearing a navy blue suit with a U.S. flag pinned to his lapel. People are going in one at a time to meet him. There are several other people…OMG, he did it! Michael brought Biden! Michael and Joe Biden are standing in front of you. Michael is explaining communication. Okay, here he is, Vice President Joe Biden!"

Biden holds the keyboard with one hand and types with the other. One by one, his fingers transmit his message, "I love you."

Flustered, I grasp for something to say. "Thank you!" Shifting the braille computer to my left arm, I offer him my hand. He shakes it warmly, swinging our hands through the air: two, three, four, five… The handshake continues the conversation while I deliberate on a response to his baffling declaration of love.

Pressed for time and juggling dozens of environmental details, we sometimes blurt out words that touch just the edge of our intended message. I think Biden wants to convey compassion and admiration. His message roughly corresponds to the textual equivalent of a radiant smile.

Taking a deep breath, I center my voice. "Thank you very much." The simple words strain to encompass all of my thoughts.

Communication shifts back to the everlasting handshake. Six, seven, eight, nine...He gently releases my hand and it falls back to my side. The gesture expressed a deep level of kindness that I both felt and appreciated.

Ryan taps my arm. As I walk into the Blue Room, my mind keeps going back to Biden. I should have said more. Waiting for the perfect thing to say can stunt a conversation.

Beside me, Ryan starts speaking to someone in front of us. I clear my mind, silencing all my doubts. Live boldly, I remind myself.

Ryan leads the way to a tall table. As I place the braille computer on the surface, Cameron sets the keyboard in front of the president. "Hello, Haben," he types. "It's nice to meet you."

I'm beaming. "Hello!" I offer him a hand. "It's nice to meet you. I had a wonderful conversation with Valerie Jarrett, and we're wondering if you can type as fast as she can."

Cam touches her fingers to my back and shakes them in the sign of laughter. The president laughed! "She's much faster," he types.

"You're doing pretty good." I smile, trying to reassure him. "My dad types with two fingers."

"I do, too."

"You type with two fingers?" My voice rises in shock.

The room erupts in laughter.

"I'm gonna type faster now," he writes.

I stand up straighter to better assess the speed of the incoming dots.

"We're proud of the leadership you've shown. Your dad must be proud, too. That time I typed with all my fingers."

"Thank you! My dad is particularly proud of my work to highlight the benefits of accessible technology." One hand gestures as I speak; the other rests on my braille computer in case he decides to interrupt me. Patient, respectful, he hears me through. "Technology can bridge the gap for people with disabilities, and as internet services open more opportunities for people, we're going to see more people with disabilities employed and succeeding."

When I finish speaking, he slips his hand under my computer hand. My top-notch tactile reading skills immediately understand his gesture. His hand leads away from the table toward him. The gesture asks, "May we hug?" His lead into that hug feels so intuitive that I sense he has serious dance skills.

He guides me back to the table and explains, "I couldn't type a hug."

"I prefer real hugs to typed hugs."

Cam draws a huge smile on my back, mirroring the president's reaction. Cam uses simple physical signals called Pro-Tactile when she can't reach my hands, like when I'm engaged in conversation with someone who may not realize they should type facial expressions. ProTactile is one of the many things I didn't have time to teach the mysterious Ryan.

"Everybody is waiting for us," the president says. "Are you ready?"

I smile. "Ready!"

We walk together, the president leading the way through the Blue Room, through the Green Room, stopping at the door to the East Room. Ryan touches my arm and the two of us slip through the doors into the East Room.

Ryan guides gracefully, allowing his arm to flow with his stride. He even remembers to signal the steps leading up to the stage. Everything I taught him, he learned. Everything I said, he heard.

At the podium, I take a moment to position my microphone and braille computer. Braille begins to scroll across the screen: "Everyone is smiling and watching you." Michael and Cam have dashed out of the Blue Room, sped through the hall, squeezed through the crowded East Room, and turned on a second keyboard.

I pull the microphone toward me. "Good afternoon!"

"Good afternoon," the audience responds.

"My name is Haben Girma. Allow me to share a story. When my grandmother took my older brother to school in East Africa, they told her that Deafblind children can't go to school. There was simply no chance. When my family moved to the U.S., and I was also born Deafblind, we were amazed by the opportunities afforded by the ADA—opportunities won by advocates like all of you.

"In 2010, I entered Harvard Law School as its first Deafblind student. Harvard didn't know exactly how a Deafblind student would succeed—"

Laughter ripples through the room.

"And honestly, I didn't know how I would survive Harvard."

Laughter erupts again.

"Without having all the answers, we pioneered our way using assistive technology and high expectations. For my grandmother, my success at Harvard seemed like magic. To all of us here, we know that people with disabilities succeed not by magic, but from the opportunities afforded by America and the hard-won power of the ADA."

My gaze sweeps the room as I remember the pioneers who protested on streets, endured exhausting sit-ins, strapped their wheelchairs to buses, crawled up the Capitol steps, and challenged discrimination in myriads of other ways. Standing before this audience of disability advocates recharges my commitment. The kids growing up now shall have even greater access than I did.

"Through my work at Disability Rights Advocates, I strive to ensure that people with disabilities have full access to the digital world—internet services, online businesses, websites, and apps. Every day I'm reminded that as far as we've come, the drive for equality is not over.

"And now, it's my honor to introduce two leaders who work to ensure that all Americans have the opportunity they seek. Please welcome Vice President Joe Biden and President Barack Obama!"

The audience applauds. I join in, too, until a hand touches my right arm. Ryan. Collecting my braille display from the podium, I slip off the stage.

"Hey, it's Michael. You did great!!!" he types. We're sitting in chairs about five feet to the right of the stage.

"Thank you," I sign.

"Biden and the president are now on stage." Michael continues typing. "The President: Hello, everybody! (Applause.) Well, welcome to the White House. And thank you so much, Haben, for that amazing introduction, and for working to make sure that students with disabilities get a world-class education, just like you have. So please give Haben a big round of applause."

Surprise and gratitude pulse through me. I look up toward the president, then ahead toward the audience, allowing my face to express the intensity of my emotions.

"So on a sunny day twenty-five years ago—I don't know if it was as hot as it is today—President George H. W. Bush stood on the South Lawn and declared a new American Independence Day. 'With today's signing of the landmark Americans with Disabilities Act,' he said, 'every man, woman, and child with a disability can now pass through once-closed doors into a bright new era of equality, freedom, and independence.'

"Twenty-five years later, we come together to celebrate that groundbreaking law—(applause)—and all that the law has made possible. Thanks to the ADA, the places that comprise our shared American life—schools, workplaces, movie theaters, courthouses, buses, baseball stadiums, national parks— they truly belong to everyone. Millions of Americans with disabilities have had the chance to develop their talents and make their unique contributions to the world. And thanks to them, America is stronger and more vibrant; it is a better country because of the ADA. (Applause.) That's what this law has achieved."

The president's words appear on a visual screen so that Deaf audience members can access the speech. Michael watches the captions and types what he sees on my keyboard. Someday, artificial intelligence will accurately convert speech to braille in real time. Until then, I need people to transcribe speeches for me. Finding people to facilitate communication, people with strong social skills and fast typing skills, is challenging. Through time and training, I've developed a community of people who can provide communication access for me at events, people like Cameron and Michael.

Michael types the entire speech, all the way to the end. "(Applause. People are standing up.)"

Turning to Michael, I point down at my braille computer. If I stand up I might miss something. Standing and holding the device in one hand leaves me with just one hand to read, which is slow and awkward. Sitting with the computer in my lap means I can read with both hands. I want to catch everything at this momentous celebration. Every word, every description, every detail. So I stay in my seat as Michael continues painting a scene. "People look emotional. Some—"

A hand touches my left shoulder. My body recognizes the gesture from ten years of ballroom dancing. Ryan's hand asks, "Wanna join?" I leap to my feet, dropping the computer on the chair. Two steps later I'm standing in front of Ryan with my eyebrows raised in a silent question.

My eyes suddenly see someone approaching me. Someone tall. Someone exiting the stage. The president! I feel disoriented without my keyboard, but I move on instinct, offering a hand. He takes it, then kisses my cheek. I can't see his facial expressions or hear his words. Still, his message comes through. As the president walks on, Joe Biden steps forward. He kisses both of my cheeks, then disappears into the crowd.

I feel dizzy with elation. What an honor. What a gift. Our leaders acknowledged me through touch, even graciously switching from voicing to typing so we could share a conversation. Their actions stir up hope for a shift from a sighted, hearing world to a sighted, hearing, feeling world.

Sitting down, I pass the keyboard to Ryan. "Have you worked with people with disabilities before?"

"Not really."

"You did an amazing job. Thank you for all your help today. Not everyone listens when I explain how to guide, use the keyboard, and practice tactile communication. You really listened."

When he touched my shoulder, I didn't know what he wanted to tell me. The suspense felt like the first few moments of a dance. My ears can't identify the music, so I walk onto the dance floor not knowing if it's a waltz, swing, or salsa. The process of puzzling out the unknown gives me an adrenaline rush. By listening through my whole body, the dance eventually reveals itself. If we study it, the unknown becomes the known.

"It was absolutely my pleasure," Ryan says. "But you are the one who was amazing. That was an incredible speech."

I blush. "It was a team effort." People with disabilities succeed when communities choose to be inclusive. My exhaustive preparation, from writing the speech to training Ryan, propelled the presentation to success, along with the support of Cameron and Michael, the dedication of the White House, and the persistence of all the advocates who created the ADA. Disability is not something an individual overcomes. I'm still disabled. I'm still Deafblind. People with disabilities are successful when we develop alternative techniques and our communities choose inclusion.

"Ryan, what's your job, exactly?"

"I'm a pilot for the Air Force."

I nod. "How does that bring you to the White House?"

"We come here for special assignments."

"Special assignments?"

"Yes."

"Got it…" Secret protocols. Special assignments. The White House works in mysterious ways. There are only so many I can solve in one day. I gesture to the room in front of us. "What's going on now?"

"People are mostly mingling. Some are here, some are in the other room closer to the food and drinks."

Many details remain unknown. Details like the topic of the nearest conversation, or if anyone nearby looks friendly and free for a chat. I could stay seated awhile and ask for more descriptions. Reading about the world from my chair is easy. Safe. Boring. I prefer dancing to watching others dance.

"Let's go meet people."

Epilogue

San Francisco, California. Fall 2018.

Exciting news swept through the disability rights community in the fall of 2015: Scribd agreed to collaborate with the National Federation of the Blind to make the Scribd library of forty million books and documents accessible to blind readers.

The settlement brought our litigation to a close. Representing the blind community in this case alongside my talented co-counsel was an unforgettable honor. I entered Harvard Law School with the dream of using ADA litigation to increase access to digital information for people with disabilities. That dream had finally come true.

After the Scribd case, my dreams shifted away from lawsuits. Litigation holds an important place in disability rights advocacy, but it's personally not for me. Many organizations want to be accessible and just need help moving in that direction. My mission now is to help increase opportunities for people with disabilities through education-based advocacy.

In 2016, I started my own business of disability rights consulting, writing, and public speaking. Public speaking is a powerful form of advocacy. When done well, it moves people to action. My foray into public speaking began in 2004 when I shared my Mali story with classmates at Oakland's Skyline High School. BuildOn required us to do presentations for four different classrooms. My knees shook throughout that first presentation. Afterward, feedback trickled in from students and teachers. When I incorporated that feedback into my next presentation, I received a huge round of applause. By the twelfth presentation, my knees had stopped shaking. At the end of the series, buildOn was so impressed, they flew me across the country to speak at their annual gala, a large event unlike anything I'd experienced before.

An audience is a gift. The most valuable thing we can offer is our time, and speakers who respect that are more likely to connect with an audience. Over the years, my disability rights presentations have touched audiences at venues and events as wide-ranging as the Apple Worldwide Developers Conference, Dreamforce, Google I/O, South by Southwest, Summit Series, TEDx Baltimore, and universities across the world.

Connecting with people can take many different forms. Recent technological developments and a shift in our culture toward inclusion have increased our ability to forge relationships across differences. I connect with people through texting and email; through social media apps; through words and stories; through humor; through sign language and dance; through a wonderful team of friends and interpreters; and through my Seeing Eye dog.

*   *   *

Maxine, the loving Seeing Eye dog who created earthquakes in New Jersey, chased me up an iceberg, helped me walk a friend home from a bar, and guided me across the stage at our Harvard Law School graduation passed away on April 16, 2018. For nine years people called me Maxine's Mom. Some even called me Maxine. Her death shattered my identity. Picking up those pieces felt like picking up glass with my bare hands.

Her passing dealt a terrible blow to my parents. They saw Maxine as my guardian angel. Even after watching me receive recognition from the president, their fears continued to roar up whenever I traveled. They would kneel beside Maxine, look into her big brown eyes, and say, "Take care of Haben, okay?" Saba would feed Maxine *injera*, delicious Eritrean bread, even though I explained that Maxine had a sensitive stomach. Girma would sneak her Eritrean spiced steak. They lavished Maxine with food to thank her for watching over me.

She was ten years old when she experienced cancer. I miss her silly antics, her long nose that would launch my hands off a keyboard, her sweet attentiveness, and the enthusiasm she brought to each trip. The loss of someone who had touched me for nine years, spending hours each day snuggled by my feet, fur-to-skin, hurts terribly. Maxine's memory will live on, always, in my heart and in this book.

In July, 2018, I returned to The Seeing Eye and trained with a new dog. Mylo, a small black-and-tan German shepherd, guides with joy and confidence on our trips throughout the country. He hops from planes to trains with ease, moving with boundless energy. He can relax amid the bright lights and crowds of a stage, even taking a nap during one of my speeches. Mylo's sweet personality has charmed my family and friends, too. He's the only dog I know who snuggles with stuffed animal toys at night, holding one in his mouth like a pacifier. Mylo can never replace Maxine, but he is exactly what I need to navigate this ever-surprising world.

Well, Mylo *and* the Alaskan. Gordon and I advanced from climbing icebergs to climbing ice walls high above the Mendenhall Glacier. We haven't traveled up there for a few years, though. Nowadays, we mostly go hiking around the Bay Area, following up each excursion with a mouthwatering meal. Gordon learned how to make Saba's *kitcha fitfit*. Saba brings him *berbere* spice from Eritrea, and he takes care of the rest. They all know better than to ask me to cook. Many years have gone by since the incident at my grandmother's house, but I'm still traumatized by that bull.

A Brief
Disability Accessibility Guide

All of our bodies change over time. We all deserve dignity and access at every stage in our lives. Most people will need to seek accessibility solutions at some point, whether for a family member, a colleague, or for oneself. Disability is part of the human experience. We all need to engage in the work to make our world accessible to everyone. Inclusion is a choice.

Why should organizations invest in accessibility?

- **Accessibility promotes organizational growth.** Disabled people are the largest minority group. There are more than 60 million disabled people in the U.S., and more than a billion around the world. Reaching a group of this scale allows organizations to grow, increasing community engagement.
- **Disability drives innovation.** Disabled people sparked the creation of many of the technologies we use today, from vegetable peelers to email. Organizations that choose to

become accessible can benefit from the talents of disabled people.

- **Meet legal requirements.** Litigation is expensive and time-consuming. Choosing to make services accessible saves resources in the long run.

WHAT CAN ORGANIZATIONS DO TO BECOME MORE ACCESSIBLE?

- **Conduct a survey to identify physical, social, and digital barriers.** Work to remove these barriers.
- **Plan for accessibility from the start.** Designing a new service or product with access in mind is easier than trying to jury-rig accessibility after the product or service has been created.
- **Increase hiring of disabled people**—one of the largest untapped talent pools.
- **Hold regular disability training sessions** to help create a more inclusive culture.
- **Promote positive disability stories** within your organization.

TALKING ABOUT DISABILITY AND PRODUCING POSITIVE DISABILITY STORIES

How we describe disability experiences in the media can help or hurt the disability community. Positive portrayals promote inclusion, increasing opportunities for education, employment, and social integration. While we can't change our past, we can influence our future through the messages we send.

Positive Messages to Send

- **We respect and admire disabled leaders,** just as we respect and admire our nondisabled leaders.
- **We can always find alternative techniques to reach goals and accomplish tasks.** These creative solutions are equal in value to mainstream solutions.
- **We're all interdependent** and go further when we support one another.

Harmful Messages to Avoid

- **Nondisabled people should feel grateful they don't have disabilities.** This perpetuates hierarchies of us versus them, continuing the marginalization of disabled people.
- **Successful disabled people overcame their disabilities.** When the media portrays the disability as the problem, society is not encouraged to change. The biggest barriers exist not in the person, but in the physical, social, and digital environment. Disabled people and their communities succeed when the community decides to dismantle digital, attitudinal, and physical barriers.
- **Flat, one-dimensional portrayals of disabled people.** Stories that reduce a person to just their disability encourage potential employers, teachers, and other commu-

nity members to similarly reduce the person to just a disability.

- **Victimizing language.** Avoid victimizing language when describing medical conditions and other aspects of the disability experience. For example, "she is blind" is neutral, but "she suffers from blindness" encourages pity.
- **Jumping through hoops to avoid saying "disability" and related words.** Linguistic gymnastics such as "special needs" and "differently abled" perpetuate stigma. We plainly state other human characteristics. We write, "She is a girl," rather than "She has a special gender." The words we use to discuss disability should be similarly straightforward. Tiptoeing around our differences is also more cumbersome: compare, "He is a person who uses a wheelchair" to "He uses a wheelchair." Keep it simple and just say "disability" and related words.

STORYTELLING PRACTICES

- **Spotlight the voices of disabled people.** Stories about disability have a disturbing pattern of marginalizing disabled voices in favor of the voices of the nondisabled parent, teacher, or friend. Practice focusing the story's attention on the perspective of the disabled person rather than the nondisabled person.
- **Avoid assumptions.** Many disability myths are so deeply entrenched in our culture that people assume them to be true. Should you use blind, partially sighted, low vision,

hard of sight, or legally blind? Ask the person being described rather than making assumptions.

- **Challenge yourself to create a disability story without using the word "inspiration."** The overuse of the word, especially for the most trivial things, has dulled its meaning. People sometimes even use the word as a disguise for pity. For example, "You inspire me to stop complaining about my problems because I should feel grateful I don't have yours." Messages that perpetuate us versus them hierarchies contribute to marginalization. Engage audiences by moving beyond the inspiration cliché.

CREATE ACCESSIBLE DIGITAL CONTENT

Accessible digital information reaches a larger audience. Organizations investing in accessibility tap into the market of more than a billion disabled people around the world while also improving the experience for nondisabled people. Accessibility features such as captions, transcripts, image descriptions, and machine-readable text enhance search engine optimization, making it easier for disabled and nondisabled people to find and engage with digital content. The Web Content Accessibility Guidelines is a set of technical standards for making websites accessible. To design accessible mobile apps, refer to the developer accessibility guidelines for iOS and Android. Here are a few things to keep in mind for digital content.

Videos

- Provide captions so that Deaf individuals can access the audio content.
- Provide audio descriptions so that blind individuals can access the visual content. Audio descriptions are spoken narrations of actions, scene changes, text on screen, and other key visual information inserted during pauses in the dialogue.
- Provide a transcript that also includes key visual descriptions. This is particularly helpful for Deafblind viewers.

Podcasts and Radio

- Provide a transcript to ensure access for Deaf audiences.

Images

- Provide an image description near the image. The image description should communicate key visual information in one to three sentences.

Articles

- The text of the articles should be machine-readable. Machine-readable text can be read by software used by blind viewers to convert the text to speech or digital braille.

RESOURCES

- Disability Rights Bar Association, disabilityrights-law.org
- Disability Visibility Project, disabilityvisibilityproject.com
- Haben Girma, habengirma.com
- Helping Educate to Advance the Rights of the Deaf (HEARD), behearddc.org
- Helen Keller Services, helenkeller.org
- Knowbility, knowbility.org
- National Association of the Deaf, nad.org
- National Disability Theatre, nationaldisabilitytheatre.org
- National Federation of the Blind, nfb.org
- Miles Access Skills Training, blindmast.com
- San Francisco's Lighthouse for the Blind and Visually Impaired, lighthouse-sf.org
- Tactile Communications, tactilecommunications.org

Acknowledgments

Ableism continues to haunt people with disabilities, rendering exclusion the norm around the world. Very few blind students in the U.S. have consistent access to braille, and only about ten percent receive braille instruction. Countless schools choose to fight parents rather than accommodate a disabled student, and numerous employers refuse to remove barriers in the workplace. Against this backdrop, the level of inclusion I experienced throughout my life is astounding. The thriving disability rights community in Oakland and Berkeley, where I grew up, connected me to disabled and nondisabled role models. They dismantled access barriers for me, teaching me how to advocate for myself in the process. My deepest gratitude goes to the teachers, employers, advocates, friends, and all the other community members who identified and removed access barriers throughout my life. It's my hope that some day the level of accessibility I experienced will cease being remarkable, and every person with a disability, from children to elders, will live in a barrier-free world.

I started writing this book in 2017. My literary agent Jane Dystel provided valuable wisdom and guidance through the journey to publication. She introduced me to Twelve Books where Sean Desmond and Rachel Kambury supported this book through their expert editing, patience, and endless enthusiasm. Thank you for championing this book Sean, Rachel, and everyone else at Twelve, including Becky Maines, Brian McLendon, Jarrod Taylor, Paul Samuelson, Rachel Molland, and Yasmin Mathew.

My family has blessed me with love and we wouldn't have these stories without them. Thank you to Saba, Girma, TT (Yohana), Mussie, Awet, and my grandparents, aunts, uncles, and cousins. Thank you, too, Gordon.

Thank you to all my readers. Your time is a gift, and I'm touched that you chose to read my book. I want to send a special thank you to my early readers: April Wilson, Caitlin Hernandez, Danielle Frampton, Daniel F. Goldstein, David Vincent Kimel, Lisa Ferris, Liza Ghosh, Mashal Waqar, Nunu Kidane, Odunola Ojewumi, and Zachary Shore. I also want to thank Stanford-based historian Issayas Tesfamariam for his patience and generosity in answering my questions on Eritrean history.

This book is a work of creative nonfiction. The stories portray events to the best of my memory. Some minor details and dialogue have been recreated in places where my memory fell short, and some names and identifying details have been changed to protect individual privacy. Literary techniques such as compressing time have been used in some instances to help the story flow. This is not an advice book, and if you follow my example you do so at your own risk. Some of the activities described here are downright dangerous, including climbing icebergs and trying unknown cafeteria food. Stay safe out there!

READING GROUP GUIDE
DISCUSSION QUESTIONS

1. Haben spent an extraordinary amount of time considering every detail when writing this book, including which tense to use. In the introduction she explains that "unlike most memoirs, the stories here unfold in the present tense." How did this style choice affect how you experienced the book?

2. Haben details her efforts to resist gendered chores like cooking, culminating in that unforgettable meat chopping scene. What would you have done if someone had played such a prank on you? Have you ever resisted doing gendered activities? Share with the group.

3. Memoirs capture experiences from a person's life that fall under a unifying theme. At the end of this book you may have wondered why Haben did not dive into the topics of dating, marriage, or babies. That's not the subject of this book. Still, some readers expressed disappointment. Should publishers require all women writing memoirs to discuss dating, marriage, and childbearing? How can we create a future in which women who write memoirs are not criticized for failing to cover traditionally "feminine" topics? Discuss.

4. While she discusses many serious topics and events, Haben's memoir is notably lighthearted and funny. What was your favorite humorous moment in the book? How does a sense of humor aid someone who is experiencing adversity? What are some of the difficult moments in your life that were eased by laughter? Share with the group.

5. Several chapters take place in Eritrea and Mali. Haben does not feel an immediate sense of belonging in these places because her disability and American background mark her as different. How does Haben strive to connect with the people around her? How effective are those strategies? Have you spent time in a community where you did not feel you belonged? What strategies did you use to build connection?

6. When Haben meets Justin at the college cafeteria, she doesn't know his race. Several conversations in, the topic of race comes up and she asks him how he identifies. How does blindness change how a person navigates a racial society? How would your world change if you only learned someone's race after an hour of conversation with them?

7. Haben experiences a surprising number of adventures in her young life. "I prefer dancing to watching others dance." If Haben were sighted, do you think she would spend more time watching instead of dancing? What drives her to experience so much in the world? How has Haben changed your perspective and your relationship to the world around you? What are you inspired to try doing? Share with the group.

8. "The dominant culture promotes ableism, the idea that people with disabilities are inferior to the nondisabled. Assumptions like: disability is a tragedy; disabled people are unteachable; it's better to be dead than disabled." During the COVID-19 pandemic several health experts proposed denying medical treatment to disabled people at hospitals unable to treat all their patients due to scarce resources. Should hospitals prioritize providing care for nondisabled people over disabled people? Discuss your thoughts with the group.

9. "Ableism runs so deep in our society that most ableists don't recognize their actions as ableist. They coat ableism in sweetness, then expect applause for their 'good' deeds. Attempts to explain the ableism behind the 'good deeds' get brushed aside as sensitive, angry, and ungrateful." When did you learn about ableism for the first time, and how did you feel? Can you think of a time when you or someone you know unintentionally did something ableist? Describe what happened. The next time you witness ableism, what will you do? What's the best way to teach someone about ableism?

10. A potential employer at a Harvard networking event repeatedly calls Haben inspiring. Despite claiming she inspired him, Simon does not invite Haben to apply for a position at his law firm. What does the word "inspiring" mean in this context? "The overuse of the word, especially for the most trivial things, has dulled its meaning. People sometimes even use the word as a disguise for pity. For example, 'You inspire me to stop complaining about my problems because I should feel grateful I don't have yours.'" When do you think it would be okay to call a disabled person inspiring? How do you move beyond the "inspiration cliché"? Discuss.

11. Society repeatedly tells us that a disabled person who wants to become successful must overcome their dis-

ability. Haben makes a point of reminding readers at the end of the book, after describing all her success, that she is still Deafblind. Throughout this book disability is never an obstacle to overcome. What are the actual obstacles Haben overcomes? What are some examples from your life when people wrongly assumed you couldn't do something? What was the real obstacle in each situation?

12. After learning to advocate for herself, Haben now uses her skills and talents to increase opportunities and dismantle barriers facing disabled people. She strongly believes that we all have the power to create positive change. What are some of the barriers in your community? Choose one of these barriers and develop a plan to remove it. Share your plan with the group and support each other in making your community more accessible.

About the Author

Haben Girma is a disability rights lawyer, author, and public speaker. The first Deafblind person to graduate from Harvard Law School, Haben advocates for equal opportunities for people with disabilities. President Obama named her a White House Champion of Change. She received the Helen Keller Achievement Award, and a spot on Forbes 30 under 30. President Bill Clinton, Prime Minister Justin Trudeau, and Chancellor Angela Merkel have also honored Haben. Haben combines her knowledge of law, sociology, and technology to teach organizations the benefits of fully accessible products and services. Her insights help to expand our thinking, creating lasting, positive change among people and communities. Her work has been featured in the *Financial Times*, BBC, NPR, *GOOD* Magazine, the *Washington Post*, and more.

Haben was born and raised in the Bay Area, where she currently lives. She shares her latest stories, photos, and videos on her website, mailing list, and social media.

Website: habengirma.com

Mailing list: habengirma.com/get-email-updates/

Facebook: www.facebook.com/habengirma

Twitter: @HabenGirma

Instagram: @HabenGirma

LinkedIn: @HabenGirma